MEATLOAF
FOR
BREAKFAST

Bronx Logic for Building Strength in America's Youth

GERARD AZZARI

MEATLOAF FOR BREAKFAST
BRONX LOGIC FOR BUILDING STRENGTH IN AMERICA'S YOUTH

iUniverse books may be ordered through booksellers or by contacting:

iUniverse
1663 Liberty Drive
Bloomington, IN 47403
www.iuniverse.com
1-800-Authors (1-800-288-4677)

Because of the dynamic nature of the Internet, any web addresses or links contained in this book may have changed since publication and may no longer be valid. The views expressed in this work are solely those of the author and do not necessarily reflect the views of the publisher, and the publisher hereby disclaims any responsibility for them.

Scripture taken from the King James Version of the Bible.

Any people depicted in stock imagery provided by Getty Images are models, and such images are being used for illustrative purposes only. Certain stock imagery © Getty Images.

ISBN: 978-1-5320-7671-8 (sc)
ISBN: 978-1-5320-7696-1 (e)

Library of Congress Control Number: 2019908039

Print information available on the last page.

iUniverse rev. date: 06/21/2019

This Bronx logic is for the millions of children longing for the loving embrace of two parents, guiding them to achieve success.

It Takes Two

CONTENTS

PREFACE

Webster's *New World Dictionary* defines *culture* as "a cultivation of the soil; improvement of the mind, manners, and so on; development by special training or care; and the skills, arts, and so forth of a given people in a given period."

I grew up in the Bronx under the concept of TRY (take responsibility yourself), an acronym imparted to me by my parents. The culture of the Bronx—and, to a larger extent, the country—in the 1960s is difficult to frame because it was a thoroughly different time. Put simply, the culture was defined by whatever was seen and heard by people in their various places. Globalization, in the sense of connectivity in economic and cultural life, hadn't happened yet. People knew only what they saw and heard in their immediate environment. To that end, the defining qualities and events of the '60s, from my perspective, were as follows:

- golden age that never was, big government, space exploration
- wartime, civil rights movement, radical activism, protests, campus riots
- racial divide
- drugs, hippies, Woodstock
- British invasion and musical stream

It was a nascent time that melded into the '70s organically. The events and qualities that defined this period were as follows:

- the '60s rebellion; conservative populism; Watergate
- fight for equality; crime and urban decay; racial turbulence

- save the environment; musical cascade continues
- international political turmoil; significant economic stress
- technological development; TV
- social transformation; movement toward higher education
- the Bronx and other NYC boroughs burn

The 1960s and '70s encapsulate the time I consider to be my growing-up period. So let's skip the 1980s, 1990s, and early 2000s and fast-forward to today ... 2018. The Bronx is still one of the poorest, most diverse, and most dynamic boroughs in the country. The country is mired in political discord and unrest; parental division persists; global terrorism and mass shootings are common occurrences; wartime, civil rights protests, and radical activism are ongoing; the racial divide continues; and we constantly hear stories about drug epidemics and violence. There have been positive developments, however, so let us not overlook them. There has been obvious economic growth across the world, partially due to technological advancement, and humans are more conscious than ever about actively preserving the environment. From my birth to date, I have seen a lot, and the culmination of what I've learned formed the idea for this book.

The actual words on these pages were formed by numerous discussions with my wife and children about growing up in the Bronx as a child. The framework and specificity took shape when eliciting input from several experienced Bronx mentors on the need to seriously engage people on the importance of having two parents available during childhood development. Why is it important for our children to be raised in two-parent households? In answering this question, I'll start with my life.

While my overall confidence developed early on, I would never have imagined that I would become a tenured senior vice president of sales and corporate officer for a subsidiary of a Fortune 500 company. I attribute my achievements, first and foremost, to the fact that I was raised in a loving two-parent household. As an adult, my success has been strengthened by the support of my wife and children, family, friends, and mentors. I am grateful for the way my parents raised me, and I am proud of my accomplishments. I continue to communicate the essence of my Bronx experiences with my children and others so they can better understand the importance of personal contribution, creating value, and building self-confidence to achieve their very best.

My brother Geoff worked in the Bronx, New York, educational system as a teacher and coach for more than three decades, and several good friends, including Dwyer, have committed to the profession for many years. As educators, they have recognized student fulfillment where parental support was entrenched and have witnessed the challenges children face in the absence of a firm parental base. They also understand that every child has the potential to succeed, regardless of a parent's marital status.

My relationships with many people from the Bronx continue until this day, and dozens of us gather weekly at a few core eateries to discuss family, work-related issues, and general topics of the day. Such discussions are free-flowing, and those individuals who engage in them work across multiple disciplines. One topic that always piques the interest of many is the degradation of the family unit, and that is what prompts the parallels of how it was in the '60s and '70s, compared to the realities today. We speak about what it was like when we were children, living and learning in a vibrant yet restless community. We opine on what can be done to resurrect a meaningful dialogue that prompts people to action, sparks a movement, and creates heightened awareness within every sector for the need for greater parental guidance.

We ponder why people today, at every level within society, tune out when discussions surface regarding the promotion of nuclear families and the requirement of two parents supporting childhood development. The group of friends and family members I mentioned above is diverse in every way. They present open views on sports, race relations, politics, their professions, and national issues that impact communities. One example where we reached a consensus pertains to the need to preserve intact families. What we recognize in various professional settings is that when the topic of family unity surfaces, people are reluctant to engage. Most repel the discussion. Do those who refrain think it is just the norms of the time and not much can be done? Do those who refuse to discuss the matter come from broken homes?

We see similar reluctance to address family division in the news. Rarely do we see meaningful press on the rate of marital dissolution and the impact on children. One example that left an impression on me was when I was watching a CNN broadcast on February 26, 2018. In the wake of the devastating shooting at Marjory Stoneman Douglas High School in Parkland, Florida, the host had former senator Rick Santorum on the show to discuss what can be done about mass shootings and gun violence. When the senator brought forward his strong views that family breakdown was a primary contributing factor for community violence, the host squelched his view and redirected the topic back to guns as the driving force. Clearly, there should be tighter gun laws, beyond passive background checks, to deter such mass violence. Yet to simply brush off the fact that individuals from broken families who commit significant acts of violence also represent a real factor is fundamentally disingenuous. In essence, the senator was censored for his views on the decline of nuclear families. This type of muffling is all too common. And the disengagement on the topic is what we react to. Why the dissociation with the value of intact or nuclear families?

They are hesitant to connect and disengage. They are deterred from any prolonged discourse that elucidates the challenges our youth face, examination of the supporting facts, or offering of potential solutions. What we witness now is a benign reaction to a cyclical malignant distortion of family values. Are the reasons rooted in new generational norms, avoidance of responsibility, political nuance, state policies, cultural disorientation, educational dysfunction, or spiritual void? The answer is *all* the above.

Try to read, view, or listen to media outlets regarding the topic of divorce and the impact on children. Any substantive dialogue on the topic is muted. In fact, the topic of divorce receives a whisper of coverage annually. As example, the Atlantic/Aspen Institute American Values Survey of 2013 had divorce at 2 percent as one of the most divisive social issues reflected in big news stories, compared to political dissonance at greater than 30 percent. Similar data on family values persist today.

Society has become immune to the extreme. Social media and the entertainment industry are a haven for exploiting and glorifying relentless, self-driven behavior. In defining this term, we need only look at the culture around us—more tangibly, the expression of the culture we see and hear each day, a culture rooted in self, manipulation for personal gain, personal satisfaction, and personal triumph at any price.

Have you observed the substance of what is put forward by the entertainment industry and media outlets across the country today? Themes absorbed by our children are less than meaningful and are filled with an egocentric reality. Examples of reality shows that capture the attention of our youth today include *Keeping Up with the Kardashians*, *The Bachelor*, *The Bachelorette*, *90 Day Fiancé*, *Love & Hip Hop*, *The Real Housewives of* [Whatever], *Teen Mom*, and *Temptation Island*. The quality that links all of these shows is the depiction of shallow personal desires; materialism; self-absorbed, dysfunctional relationships; and weak human spirits.

Is this valuable, constructive entertainment or education for our young to embrace? Is this the best we can do to portray what *reality* is in America today? Are you kidding me? Cable shows consistently highlight fragile family structure and anemic values. The more bizarre and extreme the show, the more attractive. Anything goes, and caretakers are paralyzed and succumb to acceptance of behavioral extremes because they attribute aberrant behavior to the norms of the times. Today, extreme behavior equals social acceptance and recognition. Weakened parental supervision coupled with unfiltered media bombardment is conditioning the behavior of our youth toward self and dysfunction.

People are more than tired of the circuitous discussions that lead to nowhere, with no action, and a prolonged acceptance of a glaring stain that erodes the fabric of our society. We need to aggressively broadcast what the voluminous data reflects in not having two parents involved in childhood nurturing. And we must also understand and communicate the favorable benefits of having intact families and parental union. To that end, an alternative orientation for learning can center on the impact of fractured families and how we can build strength in the youth of America.

We know the cause of childhood disillusionment, but any limited conversation remains embedded in the *symptoms* of parental separation. Symptoms may include but are not limited to

- shallow educational performance,
- low self-esteem,
- poverty,
- violence,
- self-degradation,
- substance abuse, and
- spiritual emptiness.

The logical and apparent *cause* is centered in either the choice of not forming a parental union or the voluntary dissolution of parental attachment. In each case, careful consideration and energy needs to be channeled toward solutions and actions to curtail willing parental disengagement.

While there are no absolutes regarding the parenting process, having a mother and father involved throughout childhood development yields primary advantages for children by preparing them for adulthood, equipped with strong self-confidence, willingness to learn, social capabilities, and readiness to earn employment. Even when there is dissolution of marriage, with careful coordination and collaboration by both parents, a child can develop favorably and achieve.

Relationships are never static, and preservation of parental unions will always be tested. Having two parents supporting the development of their children into adulthood has been a societal challenge for many decades, as reflected in the current rate of divorce.[1] However, when parental bonds are not formed consciously, leaving children vulnerable, that raises a different domain of rationale and represents a significant societal weakness.

As noted, we understand that every child has the potential to learn and develop into a productive adult in the absence of married parents. There are millions of children in our country who are tested to achieve, even though their parents are not united. As a point reference, each year the Census Bureau captures the living arrangements of US children through its Current Population Survey. The most recent data I reviewed from the 2014 census data reveals that, for example, twenty million children lived in single-parent families. Under such arrangements, a child is not cohabitating with both parents and is therefore dependent upon each parent to provide support and guidance independently.

I appreciate and acknowledge the unfiltered communication and genuine interest I receive during my discussions with my numerous longtime Bronx friends, people who have built solid careers within the NYC educational system, legal system, law enforcement, social services, and health care system. Each well-informed collaborator has presented a unique perspective based upon his or her expertise and encounters with our youth, bridging eras. I am always willing to listen and learn from those who are informed and can provide novel insights into challenging matters that affect people in every community in a substantial way.

We are confident that with genuine enlightenment of the requirement to dramatically enhance the development of America's youth, we can attract hordes of ambassadors—people in all facets of society who will take a stand and speak out for preserving the rights

---

[1] From the 1970s through 2016, the divorce rate has averaged approximately 50 percent, according to the US National Center for Health Statistics.

of children living with two parents. Let's all acknowledge the blatant need, and offer solutions that enable parents, educators, community and religious leaders, and political activists to lead social change toward this critical familial objective.

What could be more important than uplifting the young within our country?

ACKNOWLEDGMENTS

I am eternally blessed with a bond of love, devotion, and respect for my wife, Susan, and my children, Daniel, Amy, and Emily.

I am forever grateful for the selfless love my parents provided to me and my family.

I am spiritually indebted to my sister and brothers for their love, instruction, and protection.

I am thankful for the willing support and mentorship I received from countless dear friends who continue to inspire me to achieve.

INTRODUCTION

Growing up in a Bronx housing project in the '60s and '70s was a unique, dynamic, challenging, and fulfilling experience—a time capsule chock-full of interesting education and life lessons that helped place me (and countless others) on a developmental trajectory to achieve success; or at the very least, to have the *opportunity* to achieve, regardless of the circumstances that presented within our community.

When a child is born, most parents have the same positive thoughts, emotions, and aspirations for that child, and they feel that having a child to love and cherish is a blessing to be embraced and nurtured for a lifetime. I was raised in a different time, when societal priorities were different than they are now. One might even say they were purer and more wholesome. Children experienced joy, and parents had a favorable outlook for their sons and daughters. How can we maintain that same dynamic today when we consider what lies ahead for our children? How can parents provide a pathway for their children to achieve their very best? This guide will provide you with a simple framework made up of three core values that are the essence of parenting:

1. Respect for self and others
2. A desire to achieve goals
3. Taking pride in oneself

When my children were little, they, like most youngsters, were inquisitive. They would ask a barrage of questions to gain information and learn about our childhood, our families, how I met their mom, and what it was like growing up in the Bronx. I enjoyed the conversations and was pleased that they were consistently curious. Dialogue within the family was a daily occurrence (prior to the iPhone explosion), yet during the week, there was plenty going on with work, school, and after-school activities, so lengthy discussions were limited.

What my wife and I enjoyed most was the union and forum chosen to communicate freely. In most instances, these impromptu discussions took place on Saturdays, sitting around a table when sharing a meal at home or in a variety of locations in the Bronx and Westchester counties in New York. Most of the time, we chose breakfast to kick off the inquisition. One place the kids liked to go was M&R Delicatessen, located in Mount Kisco, New York. They knew what they wanted and got to know the staff over time. Their choice was some sort of egg sandwich, yogurt, muffin, fruit, or bagel. My wife would pick at something, and I settled on meatloaf on a roll with brown gravy. I loved it. There is no better way to jump-start your weekend and get your arteries hopping. Our discussions over a meatloaf sandwich represent the personal origin of this youth-development guide.

This guide represents a framework for what came before and after those discussions with our children. *Meatloaf for Breakfast* will help you communicate with and direct the young ones in your life to help them grow into loving and successful adults. Those family gatherings over breakfast lasted for a good ten years, until the children were well versed on our past and our vision for supporting them as they developed. At some point, they became restless and bored and accused us of repeating things. In reality, they grew into other interests, including sports, being with friends, and doing what kids do when they don't want to hear parents anymore. In any event, the decade that we spent sharing stories, connecting, laughing, and crying gave us a unique perspective on learning the three core values I listed above.

By the way, this is not a revolutionary schematic about child-rearing. Rather, this novel composite and compass on childhood development recounts my experiences growing up in the Bronx and reflects on how those experiences informed my adulthood. I share this book with you with the intention of helping children to thrive in any circumstance, in any community. The viewpoints outlined in this guide represent an amalgam of my pronounced observations and experiential learning since childhood. I do not have expertise on the subject matter. I do not have a master's degree in education. I do not have a PhD in childhood development. I have not received formal instruction related to parental guidance, nor have I acquired any distinct learning in the social sciences.

What I do possess are keen insights into the extraordinary value of having two parents, family, and community mentors carefully guiding the young into adulthood. My awareness of the topic is built upon a strong base of interactions with hundreds of families living in and around a Bronx housing project. Forming meaningful bonds with hundreds of other students throughout my educational experiences shaped unique perspectives on adolescent development. Engaging in team sports in school and within the community offered tangible learning that supported the modeling of key behaviors that attribute to attainment of goals. Working within the social-service arena and pharmaceutical space gave me a clear view of the significance of leadership and motivating others to experience the rewards for achieving goals and objectives and helping others develop skills to achieve and maintain a drive to excel independently. Strong leaders are able to create a vision and plan for others to follow in order to be successful at life.

Such life experiences and connections with thousands of individuals from all levels of the social spectrum, spanning over a half century, helped me recognize and appreciate the importance of having caring parents and social leaders dedicated to the development of others. Having two parents gave me the guidance and support I needed to build the self-confidence to lead and achieve, and I believe that the skills and leadership I gained from growing up in a two-parent household is reproducible, even in today's less-wholesome environment.

Meatloaf for Breakfast is a guide that offers a reasonably sound approach and personalized Bronx logic for building strength in America's youth. This guide can assist you in navigating the young toward achieving the highest level of personal growth, regardless of barriers that may exist in a community. You can gain insight into how to provide structure and build strength for the children you are responsible to nurture, develop, and lead. It can be a valuable reference tool for adults who work with our youth within high schools, colleges, universities, and community outreach programs and for every adult who comes into a child's life and has a meaningful influence on that child's development. Most important, however, are the parents, for their influence is paramount. So if you are a parent (or are planning to become one) to little ones you are raising in a traditional two-parent household, this book is for you.

I am confident you will appreciate and remember these important messages so you can begin to communicate and shape your plan to help support and guide the young ones you love and respect in peace!

Blessed are the peacemakers ...

~

Developing and supporting the young in America is our primary responsibility. It's important to recognize that children living in the absence of two parents can be weakened by the challenges they are sure to face throughout their childhood and adulthood. Our youth define our future, and we have a great opportunity to set them on the right path to succeed.

Children who grow up in the twenty-first century face an environment packed with more than enough roadblocks and opportunities, and we, as mentors, educators, and leaders, must do our part to set our young on the path toward the personal reward of achievement.

Our collective aim in building strength in America's youth centers on creating a cultural paradigm shift away from a cavalier indifference for child-rearing[2] and migrating toward a fulfilling, selfless commitment to all phases of childhood development. We have

---

[2] Parents today, in my view, focus more on their own needs and desires, and child-rearing is secondary.

an opportunity to trigger a *new cultural tipping point*, where individuals respect and embrace the sanctity of life from birth to maturity.

While we continue to grow in numbers, our society has regressed and has become murky in many respects. Thousands of acts of human kindness are displayed around the country each day, yet these wonderful deeds are darkened and overshadowed by the numbing evil we see all too often in our own communities. Even with the presence of a prevailing evil, we have the capacity to express gratitude and good will *when we choose to.*

A galvanized human spirit reveals itself passionately when our country experiences significant trauma. We do not hesitate to rally together with great strength during times of stress and extreme anguish, when our country, a group, or an individual is attacked and killed. For example, the horrific events of 9/11 that many witnessed remain branded in our minds. We recall the horror that unfolded, the loss of life, and the courage, bravery, and heroism put forward by hundreds of men and women who gave their lives so others could live. We ponder the multiple wars that followed in Iraq and Afghanistan and have learned of the ultimate sacrifice given by our soldiers fighting to support our freedom—and that recognition still carries through today. Through the trauma and strain we witnessed, we grew together and were motivated to overcome and heal as a nation.

We mourned in unity for the innocent life taken by an individual tormented by mental disease, unveiled through violence at Sandy Hook Elementary School. We can go on and on recounting the pain inflicted throughout our country in decades past and revisit the same feelings with new accounts that surface each day. Some acts are more egregious and revolting in nature, but they all involve evil expressed in violence toward another. Evil is ever present, and the only antidote to keep it at bay is the preservation of a peaceful faith, expressed in loving acts of kindness toward others. Because of the pain and suffering we have endured throughout the ages as a nation, we have become more resilient and hardened to the evils that are revealed each day.

We all unite in times of turmoil, so why, then, are we reluctant to bring forward the generosity of the human soul each day, when interacting with our families and communities? We all have the capacity to maintain harmony and give of ourselves freely to support others in need. We just need to release and broadcast positive energy to those we influence and encounter.

The presence of evil reveals itself in the hearts and minds of the weak and vulnerable and those lacking support, guidance, and understanding of the importance of sharing peace and harmony. Bringing forward a revelation of responsibility and kindness in our world begins with nurturing the young. Instilling a foundation of character, respect, and pride in children in every community in America will have a mesmeric effect in warding off evil and will free our young to explore the richness life has to offer. That's our goal, and it is not a new one to proclaim. We all want the best for our youth, yet obstacles get in the way of bridging the free union between parents and their children. There are lots of distractions, beyond those we impose on ourselves, that detract from the focus of developing our children. We can all cut through the clutter if we choose to. If we want to create a more balanced and vibrant future for our youth, we need to change our approach and commit to doing what is right for them.

Now, imagine that you left earth in 1978 for a four-decade exploration of our solar system. When you return to earth, you begin to acclimatize to your new reality. What's changed? Primarily, you'll find it's the speed of information. The second you land, you will first be overwhelmed by a sophisticated and swift media frenzy that will try to interpret your intentions for leaving earth in the first place. They will or won't listen to your answers, form their own biased views on the matter—not simply the news or facts—and nationally broadcast them. Then, you will learn about social media and the internet, which is largely responsible for how rapidly information is transmitted and subsequently spread throughout the world. You will learn that what is labeled *social media* has morphed into "antisocial media." You will find that real or meaningful communication between earthlings no longer exists.

You will discover the augmented entertainment industry and reality TV and its contorted impact on the youth in America. You will understand that "nonreality TV" is recognized by our youth as a generational norm and as mainstream as you can get. You will realize that the family structure that you may have been accustomed to has now blended into a normalized orientation to *whatever society wants it to be.*

People regularly absorbed in a religion that espouses peace and love are suspect. Faith and family are grouped as wishful thinking and planted in a bucket of hope. You have landed in a society where the climate now reads "anything goes." There are no limits on what's acceptable behavior; there are no restraints; there is little regard or adherence to laws; and authority is in the headwinds. Immediate self-gratification gives meaning to life. And with all that change, you will also be disheartened to find that you are still living under a national flag of division, sowed by chronic racism, violence, generalized bigotry, governmental disorder, and educational erosion. Most of all, you will find a lot of broken families.

My friends, you have landed in a time warp wrapped in a ball of confusion. But what has really changed since you departed? Not much; just a few mishaps and societal manifestations of what reality should be. The real issue at hand is the overwhelming recognition that the *human species is absolutely flawed.* This is not a sudden revelation; this fact has been apparent from the beginning of time and is defined in the book of Genesis. The challenges and human weakness we cultivate in our society are a reflection of the frailty of the human spirit.

Adam and Eve did as they wanted and defied the Creator of the world. They were given freedom of choice, and so it carries on for millennia. The realization that freedom of choice, when compounded by the prevailing presence of evil, leads to chaos and weakness is not readily understood. But it needs to be. We need to accept that we are not perfect and then make an effort and take responsibility to improve our lives by focusing on others, not ourselves and our immediate wants and desires. *Faith and family* is not a tagline. Together, they represent the bedrock for our nation, and we will make the effort to reinstall the virtues of love and respect for others.

Specifically, we need to do everything we can to safeguard children growing up in a society that advocates peace and happiness. Our children have the right to live in an environment where parents are committed to their development. We have the ability to create change in our respective communities, and that change starts with a concentrated effort to build confidence and competence with the young in our lives. Making the right change is not something to "hope for." Hope is vague and intangible and not definitive. Our society requires an immediate remedy and steadfast commitment to aid the young in achieving their goals peacefully, for a society is a reflection of its members. Children who are not raised with two ever-present parents may find it difficult to thrive and become driven, independent, virtuous, and successful members of society.

Malcom Gladwell notes in his heralded book *Tipping Point—How Little Things Can Make a Big Difference* that it does not take many people to start a tipping point. "The tipping point is a movement of critical mass, the threshold, the boiling point."[3] He likens a tipping point to an epidemic. He comments that "epidemics create networks … a virus moves from one person to another, spreading through a community, and the more people the virus infects, the more 'powerful' the epidemic is."[4]

Gladwell specifies that it takes people with special social skills to connect and "for a social epidemic to start … some people are actually going to have to be persuaded to do something."[5]

Let's create a tipping point, a social contagion that focuses on building up the youth of America. Teaching our young to respect life, live in peace, and develop a creative passion to achieve is a tipping point worth igniting. Let's reprioritize our children. Let's offer them the support and love that only the presence of two parents throughout childhood can give. Let's remember who we are and what's important, and get back to creating a just and harmonious society.

---

[3] Malcolm Gladwell, *Tipping Point: How Little Things Can Make a Big Difference* (Little, Brown and Company, 2000), 13.

[4] Ibid., 271.

[5] Ibid., 69.

CHAPTER 1

Parental Structure: Love of a Mother and Father

S tarting a family and keeping a family intact is a parent's dream. I can say without hesitation that the Bronx family unit in which I grew up was strong, loving, and formative. My parents provided the necessary structure that served as my home, centerpiece, and supporting foundation.

As the youngest of five children, I had the opportunity to learn from the mistakes of my siblings. I quickly learned if I stepped out of line in any way, I would be reprimanded. I was expected to act and behave in a manner my parents would respect. I became acutely aware of pitfalls and how to address situations I encountered. Mischievous, curious, active, distracted, fun-loving, attention-grabber, troublemaker, royal pain in the ass—these are a few words I heard to describe my approach to learning each day. Nonetheless, they were my default methods of getting into things and trying to experience what was out there. I was constantly testing the limits of what I could get away with and learned the hard way what "don't cross line" meant.

My parents had four other children to care for, and they did the best they could, based on what they had learned from previous generations. Both were strong-willed and loving and always put their children first, regardless of circumstances. Raising a large family was not easy. Both of my parents worked, but it still was a challenge to make ends meet.

Making ends meet meant paying the rent on time for a family of seven in a three-bedroom apartment. It meant having the kids wear the same clothes when hand-me-downs were not available. Making ends meet meant paying grammar school, high school, and college tuitions. Having a bigger family meant bigger food bills, especially with four boys with voracious appetites. Not an easy task for my parents to keep a family afloat, but they did. And they did so willingly.

During the '60s and '70s, sacrifices had to be made, and we just learned to adjust and adapt. We had no car. Public transportation was commonplace and the only way to get where you were headed. Our clothes were not the most pristine, but they were presentable. Thank goodness for school uniforms in grade school. Many times, the food purchased for the family was by credit, which meant "on account" (on account of we had no money) and was paid over time.

Many other sacrifices were made, such as not being able to attend family functions often because getting to the event would cause hardship. Having to eat simple one-dish meals to fill us up was routine. Some of my favorite dishes today, however, are those that we grew up on. Pasta or macaroni was a staple and the best filler known to humankind. Not a big hit today because of the low-carb craze, but it can calm and curb the appetite of even the largest human. This is especially true when the right dish is prepared. Though my mother wasn't a cook by profession, she learned by doing, and she became a really good one. She made delicious dishes like pasta e fagioli, pasta e broccoli, pasta e ceci, and pasta e piselli. These were go-tos, but there were other variations that always satisfied.

So that's the story. All you need in life are well-intentioned, loving parents who clothe and feed you, pay your bills, provide discipline, and encourage you to make sacrifices so you can grow and achieve. Now, that may not be the whole story, but it's a damn good place to start.

IT TAKES TWO

Most of the families and friends that I grew up with had a firm base, with two parents. Where we grew up in the Gun Hill housing projects, many of other families also had both parents. More specifically, within an urban housing complex in the Bronx, New York, during the '60s and '70s, there were literally hundreds of families raised with a similar parental structure.

The projects, within the one square block where I lived, had six buildings, each containing fourteen floors with nine apartments on each floor. That's 756 low-income, diverse families, living in close quarters, all shared a similar learning experience since birth. Two parents making similar sacrifices for their children led most of those families—same experience, regardless of whether they were white, black, Hispanic, Asian, Catholic, Jewish, or any other faith. Cultural differences, perhaps, but a family's race or religion was irrelevant. The experience of having a strong parental base was almost universal.

Such an experience was not limited to the projects. Almost all the children we knew in "the neighborhood" had their parents to guide and direct them during their childhood. There was a paucity of friends who did *not* have both parents early on, and those youngsters who suffered the adversity of losing a loved one had to lean on the surviving parent heavily, to compensate for their emotional loss. In the rare instance where both parents had passed away, siblings or relatives stepped up to provide guardianship. Additionally, having parents separate or divorce was sporadic at best during that time period. Even in those infrequent instances, both parents were still available to play a key role in the child's development. Perhaps it wasn't as structured an environment as having both parents under one roof, but each parent was accessible nonetheless.

We learned what we could from our parents, and the knowledge gained was appreciated, though not always accepted. Everything that went on around us at the time seemed impermeable, as long as we had the protection, support, and guidance from our parents.

Growing up so closely with other families during the '60s and '70s was a blessing in itself. Even though the environment was plagued with difficulty and turmoil—racial divide and an ongoing, unpopular war—we had the peace, strength, and unity of a larger family embodied within the projects. Racial tensions, financial woes, war effects, drug infiltration, and governmental disarray seemed checked. A common thread rooted in the parental core softened the environmental burden.

There were plenty of discussions on matters that surrounded our society at the time. Most of the issues were debated primarily in the household, and many were brought forward in smaller groups with friends or in school. We all learned from each other and respected views that might not have aligned with our own. That aspect, in itself, was a valuable learning experience to draw upon over time.

But fundamentally, as with all children, my learning had its roots in who my parents were.

WHERE IT ALL BEGAN

My father, Hugo Armando Azzari, was born in 1907 and grew up in Harlem, New York. He was a second-generation Italian American from the town of Carrara. Located a couple of hours north of Rome, this settlement represents an area in Tuscany noted mostly for its gorgeous terrain, climate, wine, and quality marble. He was the eldest of eight children and son of Enea and Ciro.

Leaving such a serene domicile in Tuscany must have caused great consternation for my grandfather Ciro Azzari. At age twenty-four, he departed from Genoa, Italy, on October 6, 1898, and sailed on the SS *Werra* with other steerage passengers, arriving in the Port of New York on October 20. Like millions of others, he wanted to come to America to create a better opportunity for himself and his future family. As referenced in the book *La Storia: Five Centuries of the Italian American Experience* by Jerre Mangione and Ben Morreale, "the heart of the story is the mass migration that took place between 1880 and 1924, when a whole culture left its ancient roots to settle in towns across America. There it was transformed and woven into the fabric of American life."[6]

He joined his brother shortly after he arrived in New York and eventually settled in Vermont. Soon, he was working side by side with

---

[6] Jerre Mangione and Ben Morreale, *La Storia: Five Centuries of the Italian American Experience* (HarperCollins Publishers, 1992), xiv.

his sibling as a laborer in a marble quarry in the town of Proctor. His skills and love of working with marble were transferred from a small province in Tuscany and advanced in a little domain in Vermont. Eventually, Ciro found his way to New York with his wife, Enea, and their offspring followed. Work and finances were tight, and the family later transitioned from 116th and Pleasant Avenue in Harlem to the Bronx, where the living space and work opportunities were more accommodating uptown on East 226th Street.

As the firstborn in a large household, my father became the surrogate parent for his parents, who spoke little English. As such, he shouldered the responsibility to earn, teach, guide, and discipline his younger siblings. His head-of-the-household function would reveal itself again when raising his children, many years later.

~

My mother, Katherine Favia, was a second-generation Italian American from Grumo Apulia in the province of Bari, which is the capital of the Apulia region in southeastern Italy, along the Adriatic Sea. Bari is a port city with fantastic universities and magnificent cathedrals that blend favorably in an urban setting. To the joy of its residents, Bari's cuisine is based on three important ingredients—wheat, olive oil, and wine—which grow well because of the rich soil and climate. I would suspect that, considering the ingredients, pasta and other wheat-based derivatives are plentiful.

My childhood friend Mario, whose family also emigrated from Italy to America, informed me of a popular saying in Bari city, "Se Parigi avesse il mare, sarebbe una piccola Bari," which translated means, "If Paris had a sea, it would be a little Bari." Seems like a magnificent place to live or visit and absorb its tranquility, and I saw pieces of that tranquility in my mother's nurturing. I wish Mom could have spent some time there, enjoying the peace and serenity that the environment provides.

My grandfather Francesco Favia also made his way to New York to seek employment and settled in the Bronx. He married my grandmother Angela, and they raised three kids in an apartment on Allerton Avenue in the North Bronx. My mother was the eldest child. She and her siblings were fortunate to be raised with both parents, but that was short lived because my grandmother died at age forty-two from a brain hemorrhage. Losing their mother at an early age created an emotional void, one that was hard to fill because their father had to work many hours to support the family.

Frank was an iceman. He delivered blocks of ice to apartment houses and served a key role in preserving meats and dairy for many families. Then, after his hands became numb, and he raised some capital, he made the leap to opening a candy store on Crescent Avenue in the Bronx. This was not a wise decision because his demeanor was beyond laid-back. Regardless of what was going on around him, he always maintained a steady state. Theft was one of the primary reasons for the demise of his business. I guess candy was in demand, and he had no interest in chasing thieves. Consolidated Edison (Con Ed) was the next stop on his employment train. This was a stop that suited him well for some thirty years, until retirement.

A few years following his retirement, Frank and two of his children migrated to California. Their departure left my mother alone in New York to raise a baby—my sister, Nancy. My mom was married briefly to a twenty-two-year-old professional boxer, whose career was cut short when he was shot and killed in a small after-hours club in the Bronx. Speculation was that he was taken out after refusing multiple requests from local influencers to take a dive. The article, appearing in the *Daily Mirror* on November 21, 1948, indicated that he was targeted before the fatal incident.

So having to nurture a baby at age twenty-one, with little to no parental or familial support, made for a trying time for my mother. I can only imagine the mental trauma that ensued following her loss and isolation. These challenging events would have long-lasting effects for many years. Mental strain, stress, and anxiety were chronic undercurrents throughout her life.

A couple of years later, she met my father. A forty-one-year-old bachelor meeting a young widow with a baby girl must have made for great conversation when they were introduced to each other at a New Year's Eve party. Their introduction clearly left a lasting impression because my parents were married on my mother's birthday, May 5, in 1951. Soon thereafter, four boys (Gary, Gregory, Geoffrey, and Gerard—the "Four Gs") would round out the Azzari team. As the years progressed, my mother and my sister, Nancy, would be surrounded by needy testosterone-filled males, which created a vibrant family unit.

Interestingly, my mom and dad were actually from different ends of the boot of Italy. As referenced, my father's kinfolk were from the northwestern part of Italy. My mother's genome was formed from clans along the southeastern corridor. In short, they were not aligned genetically, culturally, or behaviorally. This factor made for a complex dynamic in building a long-lasting relationship.

What I remember most about my parents was their constant focus on meeting our needs. Neither parent was centered on themselves. They had little interest in doing anything that would have them as the primary point of attraction. In fact, most parents at that time were very similar in their approach in supporting their children. It was all about the family first, no matter what.

Most parents then had little formal or secondary education. Some men, like my father, chose vocational school. Funny thing is, my father took up auto mechanics, yet he never learned to drive or lift the hood of a car after graduating. Many men were off to the military or worked when they were teenagers, if they could find employment. Some women worked full time; if they had children, they were exclusively caretakers and housewives and may have lived with their parents.

Prior to joining the navy and working at the post office, my dad worked as a laborer and machinist. He enjoyed working with stone and marble and was proud to carry on the tradition. In fact, he played a role in setting the marble in a few well-known landmarks in New York, including the Empire State Building and the Waldorf Astoria Hotel. His work was physically demanding, and the pay was not great, but it helped his family through tough times before and after the Great Depression.

My father may or may not have been aware of the deep history and association of sculpting and cutting marble that dated back centuries before he and his father ever became acquainted with such labor. In *La Storia*, there is a prominent reference to Thomas Jefferson:

> "Thomas Jefferson during his years in the White House asked the government's public architect ... to enlist the aid of his old friend Filippo Mazzei in finding Italian sculptors ... for embellishing the Capitol ... The first two sculptors to accept the invitation were brothers-in-laws, Giuseppe Franzoni and Giovanni Andrei, both from Carrara, the town famous for its marble."[7]

If my father wasn't aware of this fact, he would have been very proud to learn that some of his townsmen created exquisite marble sculptures that formed the grandeur of the Capitol of the United States.

Following his honorable discharge as a machinist's mate second class from the US Navy in December 1945, my father was able to secure employment with the United States Postal Service. He took a full-time job as a clerk, working nights at the post office on 149th Street and Grand Concourse, not too far from iconic Yankee Stadium. He took the night shift because the pay was a tad higher, and with a few mouths to feed over time, every cent mattered.

My mom was eager to work but waited until I was four years old. Either our family really needed the income, or I just wore her out, as it was not common at this time. Most mothers were housewives and caretakers. I think it was a little of both, needing the income and wanting to recharge her battery away from the house sometimes. She landed a part-time job as a sales clerk at Alexander's Department Store on the Grand Concourse in the Bronx. This large shopping depot was just a few miles north of where my dad's employment den was located.

My father would be home during the day, and my sister would chip in, watching me when she came home from school. What a treat for

---

[7] Ibid., 22.

me. Hugo had to watch me after working the night before, and Nancy, at age fourteen, was responsible for tending to me after her high school freshman day came to an end. I am sure she was utterly elated to have to take care of her little brother as soon as she put her books down. Things did pick up a bit, however, when my brothers came home from school and my mother got home from work.

My mother would leave for work around eight in the morning and walk a few blocks, where she would wait for the bus. After traveling a few miles, the bus would drop her off at the corner of Webster and Fordham Roads. This location was adjacent to the western portion of the campus of the historic educational territory at Fordham University. She would then walk up a long, steep hill for about seven blocks until she reached the Grand Concourse and Alexander's. This commute was a stimulating yet rugged trek in all kinds of weather conditions.

Following her workday, she would navigate her way home, where her second occupation would commence around three o'clock. She would grab the shopping cart and head "up the avenue" on White Plains Road to secure some provisions. Once back home, Katherine would begin her magic in the kitchen, preparing some of the most enjoyable meals any family could savor. We really did not care what cuisine was provided. Just sitting around the table, enjoying what we had and discussing the happenings of the day are some of the fondest memories I have of our family time. This routine continued for years, until the family started to thin out as a result of marriages, employment, and college attendance.

IMMACULATE CONCEPTION

Once I was of school age, a whole new arena of excitement opened up for me. I clearly recall my first day of grammar school. My father walked me across the street, past the church, and up to the doors of my kindergarten classroom at Immaculate Conception on Gun Hill Road. He let go of my hand and told me to head into the class, where the other foreigners were headed. I reluctantly moved away slowly, and as tears fell, he smiled reassuringly and retreated toward home.

I then joined in with the crying chorus of the other lost souls in a new frontier of learning. Sister Genevieve eventually calmed us or threatened us to sit at our tables. I don't remember which tactic she chose, but it worked. This went on for many days to follow, and the threats became more intense (nah, just kidding, at least for that time period), as we became more energetic and more comfortable with our second home. Some of my dearest friendships were formed during that early childhood experience—friends like Scandiffio, whose company I enjoy today, over a half century later.

When I was five years old and in kindergarten, my brother Geoffrey was in third grade, Gregory was in fourth, and Gary was on the other side of the building in seventh grade. My sister, Nancy, found her way up the street as a freshman at Evander Childs High School, also on Gun Hill Road.

As my schooling began to take root, I soon learned that having older brothers in the same elementary school provided me comfort and confidence. I was protected, and if there was any anxiety or encroachment, I had not only newfound friends to speak to but also a comfortable sibling blanket. My siblings were always available if I needed assistance, if I was wresting with an issue, or if I had questions on a matter. Most likely because Geoff was closest to me in age, he took a fervent interest in my development, and we slept in the same room, he was my primary go-to in most instances. As we aged, he became a reliable adviser, insulator, and companion. That same allegiance has been maintained over time; my relationship with all my siblings remains firm.

My education now had duality, with my primary base at home and my ongoing exploration each day in school and church. I am grouping school and church as one entity because in attending a Catholic elementary school, not only do you go to a different school than most of the kids in your neighborhood, but you inherently become indoctrinated in the fundamental tenets of the faith.

I learned plenty each day on both fronts, and I became educated mostly through observation and listening. As my parents began to age, they expected their children to always remain close and help each other in need. This is not to say that our parents let go of the reins totally in providing guidance and discipline, but they knew that there was significant strength in having their children work together to deal with challenges. The coupling of parental structure, with the choice of attending a Catholic elementary school, provided a series of learning that included, but was not limited to, understanding the importance of respect, obedience, discipline, effort, and commitment to faith. These were cornerstone expectations, beliefs, and behaviors that were taught early on and would serve as a sturdy platform for absorbing daily lessons.

Our parents stressed the need to communicate and engage each other consistently. In fact, they made it an expectation. To them, family unity and integration meant everything. Collaborating with a sibling, however, was a task in itself, as each encountered his or her own issues and did not really want to or have time to address mine. In reality, as the youngest of five, my voice was usually curbed. When I encountered situations that required explanations or input, rarely were my questions answered thoughtfully. For example, if I questioned the value of school, which I did often, as do most kids, my siblings told me, "All kids have to go to school because it's a state law, and if you don't go, you will not be able to get a job." This answer didn't resonate with me because the idea of having a job was so far in the future it seemed like an illusion. I just wanted to play with my friends. My siblings didn't offer any comfort. Hence, the methods described earlier became my way of being heard. There we plenty of trials we had to work through within the household and at school; such was the case in any household in the neighborhood.

As our family aged, so did the load of having to house and school the team. With a burgeoning family and more demands, tensions surfaced. Pressures mounted, disagreements presented, and arguments ensued between our parents, between siblings, and between parents and children. Sometimes the chatter of the day was simple needling between my mom and dad, yet some days the differences in approach were deafening. Many times, one of the siblings intervened to call off the disturbance and redirect them to more relevant issues.

The quarrels between our parents centered mostly on the financial strain of not being able to meet all the needs of our family. Even with both parents working, the income level was not adequate to sustain the essentials. As a point of reference, in 1965, our total net family income was about $700 per month, and though it was comparable to the median family income at the time in our neighborhood, for a household of seven, that amount could provide only $25 per person, per week. That included rent, food, home goods, clothes, tuition, and transportation. Finances were anemic, so we had to sacrifice in many ways to make ends meet, and therefore, many hardships were commonplace in our household. As a result, there was an ongoing request from my dad to cut back on food purchases, clothing costs, and other expenses that were required to get each family member through the day. Even though the price of goods was a fraction of what it is today, the costs were still commensurate with the economics of the time.

As example, rent for our apartment in Gun Hill projects was about $200 per month, and tuition for four children in elementary school per month was $150. Clothing for a family of seven certainly was not a low-cost ticket item. Food purchases absorbed a sizable chuck of the budget. According to the US Bureau of Labor Statistics, common staples, such as "bread was twenty-four cents a pound. Milk was twenty-five cents a quart. Cheese was seventy-two cents per pound. Fish and beef were eighty-five cents a pound, with veal at $1.74."[8] So other than occasionally eating veal cutlets, where could we cut back? In the end, we ate less of what we could afford. We scaled back across the board where we could, but rarely was there a surplus to family funds.

---

[8] "Retail Prices of Food, 1964–68, Indexes and Average Prices," Bulletin of the US Bureau of Labor Statistics, no. 1632, 45. https://fraser.stlouisfed.org/files/docs/publications/bls/bls_1632_1969.pdf.

Still, over time, fairly typical parental squabbles persisted over matters of the past and those in the present. At times, these disputes became intense. Irritation between my parents grew to a point where there was a recognizable gap in communication or compromise. Both parents were obstinate to a fault. Each could be very loving, but at the same time, their heightened stubbornness eroded any potential warm intentions.

My father wanted to bang his chest, claiming he was the one to make the calls. After all, he was the senior sibling in his house while growing up, and he wanted all to know that he would have the final say as the senior citizen of his family. Yet my mother, as Taurus the bull, wasn't having it, and she would stake her claim in all matters that pertained to the family. She never shied away from having her voice heard regarding matters that had a direct impact on the welfare of her family. This contention went on and on over the years, with interludes of tenderness, but the friction took its toll on both parents.

My mother had already come to the table with emotional strife, having dealt with traumatic events in her past, and the seasoning of turbulence only compounded her frustration. My father carried the flag of burden from his years of guiding his siblings and parents in his youth, and the discord in his relationship wore him down. It didn't wear him out, but he became softer. Essentially, there was an emotional disconnect between the two, but together they would adapt and learn to work through most obstacles.

One contributing cause of frustration between my parents was that they rarely saw each other to enjoy any quality time. They were like two ships passing in the night. When my father arrived home from working the night before, my mother would be getting ready to head out and begin her day. The only brief time they were together was with all of us at dinnertime. Sometimes Mom worked Saturdays as well, and their time together was relegated to Saturday night and Sunday. Much of that time was spent doing chores or shopping. Dad was trying to get his rest "in peace and quiet," but any downtime within the family was hardly quiet.

When we were younger, many times my father would make brief appearances outside of his room to uncover what the disturbance was and the likely culprit. He would bark at us and retreat back into his cave. If the recreational activity (e.g., music, television, aluminum-foil-lampshade basketball, football, and baseball tossing) persisted enthusiastically, he would reappear more vigorously and more animated. Most of the time, I was his target because he claimed I was the loudest. I was then put in the penalty box of my dad's room for a brief time-out and would remain there until my mom or one of my brothers retrieved me. The same shenanigans continued each day until we were old enough to remain outdoors with friends and wreak havoc, where we could participate in any number of activities.

Through all the ups and downs and dealing with what life served up, my parents remained intact. They found joy in doing what they had to do for their kids, even if it meant compromising their own relationship. Seeing their children grow older, more knowledgeable, and independent brought great happiness and pride to each of them. It was that contentment, through the education and growth of their children, that brought them closer and more at ease over the years.

What did I learn from my parents? How did I to apply what was learned? How had what I learned while observing my parents prepare me to meet the challenges ahead? These are just a few questions that come to mind in putting this educational process in play as a building block for achieving success. I learned plenty; a few key elements include the following:

- value of parental love
- logic
- mentorship
- importance of traditions
- TRY

First and foremost, I learned the value of *parental love* and its importance in understanding how to "give" willingly, regardless of circumstance, to help children develop and succeed. Second, I have tried to take a logical approach to meeting the needs of my family. Having the entire family involved in the discussion continues to be an important part of the development process. Creating a sense of ownership and accountability is an essential aspect of how we attempt to manage our affairs.

I also learned that in being a mentor, there is a responsibility to continue to uphold the traditional values of faith, education, hard work, and sacrifice. I learned that no matter what the issue is at hand, by collaborating with family members and establishing a reasonable action plan, any obstacle can be overcome and can lead to a favorable outcome. This is the same approach I incorporated into my business activities since joining the workforce as a teenager. These basic strategies and tactics have served our family well in developing the knowledge on how to take responsibility to achieve.

As referenced, if you can instill the simple word *try* into your child-rearing efforts, the learning will follow. Through education, there is understanding, enlightenment, and awareness. These principal elements of learning are an integral aspect of personal growth and development.

I am proud of my parents—how they sacrificed and made every effort for the benefit of their children. No matter what, they did everything they could to protect us, guide us, and put us in position to make the right decisions. Perhaps we made some errant choices along the way, but at least they gave each of us the support and foundation necessary to achieve success in any path we chose to blaze.

And *laughter* has always been a healing modality for my family and me, and I have made every effort to teach the same within my household. "Laugh, and the world laughs with you/Weep and you weep alone."[9] This phrase begins the poem "Solitude," written in 1883 by American poet Ella Wheeler Wilcox:

[9] www.bookbrowse.com/expressions/detail/index.cfm/expression_number/446/laugh-and-the-world-laughs-with-you-weep-and-you-weep-alone.

Laugh, and the world laughs with you;
Weep, and you weep alone.
For the sad old earth must borrow its mirth,
But has trouble enough of its own.
Sing, and the hills will answer;
Sigh, it is lost on the air.
The echoes bound to a joyful sound,
But shrink from voicing care.
Rejoice, and men will seek you;
Grieve, and they turn and go.
They want full measure of all your pleasure,
But they do not need your woe.
Be glad, and your friends are many;
Be sad, and you lose them all.
There are none to decline your nectared wine,
But alone you must drink life's gall.
Feast, and your halls are crowded;
Fast, and the world goes by.
Succeed and give, and it helps you live,
But no man can help you die.
There is room in the halls of pleasure
For a long and lordly train,
But one by one we must all file on
Through the narrow aisles of pain.

CHAPTER 2

Family Values: Faith and Family

Wikipedia, the free encyclopedia, indicates that *family values*, sometimes referred to as familial values, are traditional or cultural values that pertain to the family's structure, function, roles, beliefs, attitudes, and ideals.

Dictionary.com, Merriam-Webster, and the Cambridge English Dictionary define *family values* as the following:

- "The moral and ethical principles traditionally upheld and transmitted within a family, as honesty, loyalty, industry, and faith."[10]
- "Values especially of a traditional or conservative kind which are held to promote the sound functioning of the family and to strengthen the fabric of society."[11]
- "Values held to be traditionally learned or reinforced within a family, such as those of high moral standards and discipline."[12]

In my view, family values reflect fundamental traditions that embody a belief in a sense of communal peace with and faith in each other, revealed in the love of family and others.

---

[10] http://www. dictionary.com (retrieved September 3, 2014).

[11] http://www.merriam-webster.com (retrieved September 3, 2014).

[12] https://www.oxforddictionaries.com (retrieved September 3, 2014).

In the social sciences, the term *traditional family* refers to a child-rearing environment with a breadwinning father, a homemaking mother, and their biological children; sociologists formerly referred to this model as the "norm." A family that deviates from this model is considered a nontraditional family.

Society today would consider the interpretations of sociologists of yesteryear regarding the traditional family as archaic and out of touch with reality. Sure, we have progressed from the traditional stance over the years, and to some extent, we have transitioned for the better. However, when you carefully analyze the definitions, there are tangible rudiments that represent an expression of what was, in fact, the norm during the '60s and '70s, in my childhood experience as a Bronxite, that still exist today in many communities across the country; there remains a desire to uphold the virtues of faith, family, and the preservation of good will to others.

I alluded to the expectations and principles upheld by my parents, and I will build upon that direction. In simple terms, family values presuppose that there is an existing family structure or an intention to build a family and download values that were learned previously. For these purposes, I'm defining a family as a married mother and father with at least one child, sharing love and respect for each other under one roof.

There would be great difficulty in installing inherited family values in the absence of a family core—a mother and father aligned together, determined to bring forward a similar cultural belief system that centers on what they view as proper and true in the development of their budding family. This is where things can get a bit hairy today, as it pertains to bringing forward a cultural belief system that is individually and uniquely viewed as proper and true. What is believed to be right or wrong for one family may not be agreed upon by another, based on life experiences. Many families with varied cultures exist in every community. And each culture adopts its own belief system or traditions. There is no universal system of family values. Essentially, each family is its own culture.

However, from my perspective, growing up in an urban housing environment in the two decades following my birth was an existing, fundamental, and universal truth. And that truth was founded on the desire of two parents who were committed to teaching their children to *respect others*, expressing in words and actions what is right and what is wrong in interacting with others. After all, my parents and grandparents spent a lifetime interacting with others in close quarters, and they learned over time the consequences for decisions made in how they interacted with others.

The accepted ethical conduct and belief that you treat others like you would want to be treated is a common belief that can be taught to anyone. This Golden Rule crosses cultural, racial, or religious lines. This was a shared belief within my family and most of the families of the Gun Hill housing projects.

Part of the idiom of family values is rooted in an established system of beliefs, principles, and morals that have been inherited from those who came before, such as the core values of this book—self-respect, respect for others, and the drive to achieve. Peace and love with others doesn't hurt either. The reinforced standards and expectations that became imbedded in our minds was an understanding of the importance of self-reliance, education, hard work, community integration, and faith. In fact, faith in the teachings of the church was the shroud that surrounded all our beliefs.

We learned about the meaning of faith from our parents, at school, and when attending church. We were educated that to have faith and trust in the principles of the church was what brought peace to all of us. Having faith was a necessary support system in my family, particularly during the '60s and '70s. Commitment to family, treating others with respect, loving your neighbor, and following church doctrines were drastically challenged during that time.

Consider the confluence of circumstances of the period—the Vietnam War, civil rights protests, assassinations of President John F Kennedy and Martin Luther King Jr., and the Cuban Missile Crisis, which came disturbingly close to nuclear disaster within the United

States and Russia. The age of the hippie, drugs, and sexual promiscuity came in vogue in the midsixties.

Over time, considering all the unrest in society, I guess there was a desire to quell some of the turbulence and find peace in space. In the world of entertainment, fiction episodes came on the scene. *Star Trek* first aired on NBC on September 8, 1966, and the show's main character, Captain James T. Kirk, pronounced his five-year mission, "To explore strange new worlds, to seek out new life and new civilizations, to boldly go where no man has gone before."

In the latter part of the era, a charted mission presented by John F. Kennedy was fulfilled when he had proclaimed, years earlier, in his September 12, 1962, speech at Rice University in Houston:

> We choose to go to the moon. We choose to go to the moon in this decade and do the other things, not because they are easy, but because they are hard, because that goal will serve to organize and measure the best of our energies and skills, because that challenge is one that we are willing to accept, one we are unwilling to postpone, and one which we intend to win …

Unfortunately, JFK was not around to see Neil Armstrong first step on the moon on July 21, 1969. That momentous episode was indeed "one small step for man, one giant leap for mankind." All the drama of space-searching was meant to escape the disorder that was unraveling on earth. The untying of interactions between the inhabitants of earth were counter to the teachings of the church and family. Society was devoid of harmony, and spiritual emptiness permeated much of it.

A host of reasons caused dissention then, and fractured race relations was a palpable matter that was on everyone's minds. With the civil rights movement escalating, there was a raised awareness, especially among the youth, of the cultural oppression that plagued the black community, and this new consciousness created tension. I was in grammar school at the time, and on occasion, they locked down the school, and students were not permitted to go home. The police were in full force in the neighborhood when one of the local gangs declared "kill whitey" day. We also heard stories from friends that attended local high schools that fights were planned, targeting minorities within their respective schools. There were never any killings or major disturbances, and we all went about our business safely, but the mere description of beating or killing another because of race represented the tumult at that time. The racial dissonance swept across the country and created much anxiety.

In his song "My Hometown," Bruce Springsteen notes his recollection of the difficulty in the following verse: "In '65 tension was running high at my high school. There was a lot of fights between the black and white; there was nothing you could do."

Movies and music at the time made blatant attempts to highlight the racial divide and discrimination. Among the numerous examples were Sidney Poitier's magnificent portrayals in *A Patch of Blue* (1965), *In the Heat of the Night* (1967), and *Guess Who's Coming to Dinner* (1967). In 1964, Bob Dylan received much acclaim when he released his song "The Times They Are a-Changin'," a visceral attempt to depict a society in flux, with social injustice and political doubt. Such entertainment vehicles helped raise awareness and spark change in the minds and actions of all viewers and listeners. The entertainment industry made a concerted effort to create a tipping point toward cultural and social evolution.

The amazing thing, however, was that even with the diversity of the Gun Hill projects and surrounding neighborhood, there was sensitivity to racial conflict, so a state of control and calm existed. I believe the parents, leaders of the church, local politicians, and law enforcement played an integral role in keeping our community safe. Here again, we come full circle to the character and responsibility of the parents as community leaders.

A large part of the stability between races within our community was that we all grew up together within the same scaffold, braced in common beliefs and values. These principles centered on treating everyone fairly and with respect, regardless of the color of their skin. That's just the way it was and the way we were taught.

Our community was unique. Parents stayed married. They remained together, even though each family had their own hardships to overcome. Parents became toughened to both internal and external stresses. Sometimes the pressures would manifest in arguments, ailments, or alienation within the home, but most times parents were resilient and would not succumb to periodic strains. That was not the case in many instances outside of our locality.

In New York and across the country, according to the US Census Bureau, divorce rates rose steadily during the '60s and '70s. "The average divorce rate in the 60s was 28%, and increased steadily in the 70s until reaching 50% in 1980."[13] That was an alarming statistic. Half of all the marriages in 1980 ended up in divorce. The divorce rate remained relatively static prior to the '60s, until 1967 when divorce laws changed. Divorce continued to rise, taking a big jump in the 1970s. Sociologists claim the increase may have been attributed to "no-fault" divorce, made feasible in the '70s.

This also represented a period where a spouse could claim irreconcilable differences as grounds for divorce, making dissolution of marriage easier. Before that time, anyone who desired to end his or her marriage had to prove adultery or cruelty in the marriage. Unfortunately, the same rate of divorce has remained relatively steady since the 1980s, at approximately 40–50 percent.

It is important to note that there is no singular method of determining the actual divorce rate. Sociologists and others that study the data and its implications use various measurements, including the *raw divorce rate*, which considers "the number of marriages and divorces per 1,000 people in a population."[14] Another examination, "although not an annual rate, considers the percent of adults in a population *ever-divorced*; there is the *refined divorce rate* that reviews the number of divorces per 1,000 married woman; and there is the fancy *cohort*

---

[13] US Census Bureau, Statistical Abstract of the United States (2011), 65. https://www2.census.gov/library/publications/2010/compendia/statab/130ed/tables/vitstat.pdf.

[14] Ibid.

measure rate that is more of a projection based on a particular cohort marrying within a period of time compared to life tables."[15]

People actually delve that deep into the data. Yet regardless of how we slice the information, we come to a similar conclusion that almost half of marriages in the United States end up in divorce. This is a far cry from being united. Clearly, this is not a pretty picture; sociologists may provide insight, but they cannot offer practical solutions to curb the current rate.

The question that comes to mind, however, is if, during the '60s and '70s, marriages were dissolving at a greater rate, why were most marriages held intact within our Bronx corridor? The answer, I believe, is rooted in the makeup of the people, geography, and living quarters. When we lived in such tight confines with our neighbors, we learned that every family was experiencing similar realities. We were not isolated. There were discussions between friends and families on how to address differences and embrace relationships. Everyone knew that families harbored their own woes, and no family went unscathed. Each family had the resolve to confront their misfortunes and celebrate small triumphs. There was an existing family within a larger family.

We had strength in numbers and the opportunity to openly communicate with friends. We had the chance to speak and listen to individuals we befriended over decades. We had the assurance that our conversations were taken seriously, and we recognized a genuine interest in our plights. We discussed options for dealing with matters of concern and tried to establish an alternate path toward resolution. The discussions were reciprocal. Relationships inside and outside of the home were binding, and families wanted to remain cohesive. Other than blatant and egregious actions between spouses, marriage and family union were preserved.

Additionally, across the street from the projects was the Immaculate Conception Church. If you did not want to discuss your troubles solely with family and friends, you could always count on an ambassador

---

[15] Glenn Stanton (Witherspoon Institute, 12-16-2015). http://www.thepublicdiscourse.com/2015/12/15983.

of the church to listen. Strong relationships were formed between families and the clergy. Priests came to know all family members individually and treated each one discreetly. Faith and prayer became an everyday prescription for any prevailing malady and provided strength to endure all difficulties.

The winning combination of noble and reliable friendships and committed and devoted priests offered the potential to supplant marital erosion. This favorable dynamic was available for everyone living in the parish, regardless of race or ethnicity, and the same positive outlook for all families was embraced as a means of overcoming common troubles.

Another potent vehicle to preserve the integrity of the family unit was the extended family, including grandparents, aunts, uncles, and cousins. It was commonplace for extended family members to commiserate with the immediate family. Most of the family lived in the Bronx as well, just a few miles away or within walking distance. Gathering with and engaging each other at dinners, parties, weddings, and other important family milestone events was important for the expression of family values.

Stories of the tribulations my aunts and uncles encountered were relentlessly riveting. When they told their stories, we were locked in. We wanted to understand the circumstances they were presented with. We wanted to learn how they confronted each situation, and what the outcome was. We asked questions and listened effortlessly so that we could imagine ourselves in that different time and place. We paid particular attention to their description of wars, the Depression era, work relations, family struggles, and times of joy, sickness, and death.

The memories created have been etched in our minds forever. I recall with great clarity the animation and colorful manner in which each family member described how they confronted each circumstance. For the most part, however, the approach was consistent and included a benign, matter-of-fact articulation of, "That's just the way it was." You dealt with each event you were presented with in the best manner you could and with the knowledge or experience you had. It was that plain and simple.

Our parents, aunts, and uncles had little control over some situations, and this was reality for most families. They had little say during wartime and had to complete their time of service. Sometimes stories were shared of friends they'd met in the service and how those friends were killed in combat. They spoke of the Great Depression, the depth of unemployment, and food shortages. Getting by was not easy, and adversity was prolonged for years. Living conditions were not pleasant. Finding employment was difficult, and reliance on government assistance was a tough pill to swallow.

They were a prideful, great generation. They wanted to remain self-sufficient and participate in the workforce. They wanted to earn and support themselves and their families. What amazed me the most was how they always clung to the belief that things would get better, and eventually, the anomalies they lived through—the effects of war, the Depression, poverty—did improve.

Through the course of learning and understanding their predicament over time, we took careful note of how they were able to remain steadfast and were determined to improve their conditions. Most of all, I remember how they addressed each situation with grace, resilience, and resourcefulness.

The family gatherings were always pleasant. They were a time to share in the bonds of love and affection. There was legitimate interest in our developmental progress, and they made every effort to support our objectives by providing guidance and meaningful suggestions. Our extended family cared and wanted to feel joy in our happiness, growth, and achievements. They were always ready and available to listen, and they were a family blessing.

Of particular interest to me was their description of their relationships—how they met their spouses, how they planned to raise their children, and how they overcame adversity within their families. Each story surfaced in a different flavor, but all of them centered on how they wanted to raise a family and provide nothing but the best they could offer. They wanted to see their children grow into loving and happy adults. Considering the challenges they experienced in their developmental years, they did not want their kids to experience the same. Rather, every effort was made to put their children in an environment to learn, grow, and excel.

My parents, aunts, and uncles barely made it through secondary school, and some chose vocational school to learn a trade. Yet in many respects, they were educated outside of the classroom through the events that affected the time period that ran parallel to their development. They understood life responsibilities and had street smarts at a young age. Some would call their educational system "the school of hard knocks." Those hard knocks would pay significant dividends as they raised their families. Their education and teachings of independence, work ethic, determination, sacrifice, and faith have endured and serve as the foundation for their families.

CHAPTER 3

Social Support: Everyone Needs a Shepherd

Wikipedia describes *social support* as the perception *and* actuality that one is cared for and has assistance available from other people and that one is part of a supportive social network.

These supportive resources can be
- emotional (e.g., nurturance),
- tangible (e.g., financial assistance),
- informational (e.g., advice),
- companionship (e.g., sense of belonging), and/or
- intangible (e.g., personal advice).

Living within a Bronx housing project, by definition, meant you were part of a larger community. In simple terms, it was unescapable that your parents and others outside of your home raised you. Having a social support system meant that you had friends, neighbors, and other people, including family, available to assist you in times of need. They were ever-present and ready to provide an alternate perspective and positive outlook.

Plenty of information has been written and expressed about the value of having an established social support mechanism in place during childhood development. In the early years, all children are exposed to foreign occurrences, and encountering anything new stimulates the brain in a number of ways. Some events are favorable, and others not so pleasant. Having an existing social brace is not only comforting and protective, but it serves to enhance a child's quality of life and provides a significant buffer against adverse experiences. The one primary objective of the social sphere is to ensure that children grow in a safe and fostering environment.

We were fortunate to have a social-support comforter in the projects and surrounding community. When you think of housing projects today, you may imagine a crime-ridden, challenged neighborhood, plagued by drugs, violence, and gangs. Perhaps partly because of the time and many of the families may not have both parents in the household. Such a representation of the projects wasn't my experience.

Once we stepped out of our doors, there was always someone to meet. Either on our floor or within our building or an adjacent one, wherever we were headed, we were going to engage in some sort of activity with others.

We learned from one another because as different as our individual lives were, we shared a similar developmental experience—we had both parents, siblings, and other family members around us from early on. Layered into the mix were friends, teachers, coaches, priests, and housing police. Having an inner circle to lean on was refreshing, stabilizing, and nurturing.

Our supporting social sphere was an important element in helping to ward off the negative effects of peer pressure. Peers, especially at a young age, can have either a favorable or undesirable impact on the development of vulnerable youth. Even with the most persistent and involved guardianship, children can fall prey to the potential harsh realities, caustic influence, and relentless pressure from those they associate with. There is only so much a parent can do to safeguard the activities of their children, and having other layers available to assist is an essential component of protection and the development of decision-making capabilities.

At the same time, for me, as the youngest in my family, having a glove around me all the time was a bit confining. I was constantly given boundaries and limits for exploration. If I spoke in unfavorable, demanding tones, I was reprimanded. If I was disrespectful to a sibling, if my behavior was inappropriate inside or outside of the home, or if

I was in a fight with a neighbor, I was punished accordingly. So while stepping outside the borders was intriguing, it came with unintended consequences, and in most instances, I was brought rapidly back into the ring. Lessons learned were quick, and I made every effort not to repeat them over time.

We lived on the fourth floor of the middle building on the eastern side of the projects. We had a clear view of the backside of the building and the church across the street. We could always observe what was going on and how active the streets were. We could hear the number 2 train approach the Gun Hill station every few minutes, and it's a mystery how we became immune to the noise as the months and years flew by.

One thing that was hard to do was become bored. Something was always happening, and if there was downtime, we got into it with our siblings, or we went and "called for" a friend in one of the buildings.

There were always friends available to join us in some action or just hang out and shoot the breeze. Enjoying competition in a variety of activities became a way to release energy and learn about fair play. When we were younger, we would hang around the projects and seek to play off-the-stoop, manhunt, football, slap ball, Johnny on the pony, or box ball. There was plenty to do until we got a little older, noisier, and rougher. We would act out aggressively, and congregate in areas we were not supposed to on the housing-complex grounds. A rule within the projects prohibited playing games and causing disturbances. Playing football on the center lawn was a no-no. Shooting off fireworks was forbidden. Fights that ensued on the grounds by the flagpole were sure to attract attention. Many times we were chased away by the housing cops or warned by the maintenance men and disbursed home so we would not be fined.

My friends and I always wanted to participate in the activities with the older crowd because play space was limited, and playing on the swings and monkey bars or jumping off the rocks became boring. Trying to get involved with the "older guys" became an activity in itself. Their forcing us away became ordinary. Some of the elders would tell my brothers to keep me away from the games, and my brothers obliged forcefully. We learned to do our best to stay out of trouble, and we uncovered a new world for exercise and freedom at the Gun Hill playground.

The playground on Magenta Street was just across the way from the two southern project buildings. This newfound location became a haven for learning about sports, competition, team play, dissention, discipline, decision-making, and winning and losing. The park was a retreat for playing basketball, stickball, handball, paddleball, football, kickball, or dodgeball—and very little hockey; cooling off in the sprinklers; or jumping off the swings. We played some games year-round, including football and basketball.

The most interesting aspect of going to the park was recognizing the factions organized by age and seeing how they carried themselves in their environment. Based on your age, you had certain times to recreate. The younger kids (ages eight to ten) would get there first and go until the older ones (ages eleven to eighteen) would take over, and the oldest crew (ages nineteen and over) would join in at their discretion. This congregation opted primarily for the handball courts, as they were not really interested in other sports. They were most interested in mingling and partying in the back court.

This one location—a playground—populated by project and neighborhood residents, was a social dynamic embraced for learning. Represented were individuals of all ages and races within a similar socioeconomic framework, yet with differing orientation to the events of the time. The older you were, the more inclined you were to be confronted with the Vietnam issues, racial challenges, drugs, and whatever went along with it. The younger group, which consisted of my friends, was not yet immersed in all the happenings of the era and thus was most interested in playing sports in a safe environment and enjoying the company of others. And then there was the middle group that covered a wider range of grammar and high school–aged youth. This core represented those who socialized with the older crop and rarely interacted with the youngest. In any event, there was developmental learning available for all, and we did just that.

As a member of the youngest group, I had an opportunity for greater learning because I had a crystal-clear view of the mind-set and behaviors of every layer. I got to know each member of every segment well over the years. I became informed of their life experiences and how those experiences had shaped their paths and patterns of behavior. At the same time, I observed the attitudes and behaviors of my own family and became more aware of methods and approaches taken when navigating various circumstances. I became more in tune with the importance of observation and listening.

Family, church, school, friends, community, and sports became essential and independent forums for education, learning, and development. They represented the traditional social support system necessary to grow and achieve success in that environment at that particular time. Think about all the daily opportunities to learn from being immersed with family matters, church teachings, reading and writing, numerous social interactions, and athletic competition.

Learning, with respect to each of these practical elements, required time and effort. In fact, any aspect of real learning includes a window of time and an expenditure of energy. Learning and understanding go hand in hand, and gaining an understanding of a specific matter is a process. I would compare the process to isolated pixels coming together over time to create an impression that is imprinted within your brain. When hundreds and thousands of pixels coalesce, they form a high-definition picture that remains in your mental archives for you to draw upon as needed.

EVERYONE NEEDS A SHEPHERD

We all need someone who genuinely believes in us. We need someone who shows willingness to support us in achieving our goals. We need to surround ourselves with caring people who are capable of providing us with the tools and knowledge to propel us to achieve our very best. We all need someone to lean on, as was touchingly expressed by Bill Withers in his 1972 song "Lean on Me."

One prominent example of learning was linked to my involvement in sports. My engaging in sports took root early on as a way to blow off steam and keep occupied. Yet how I became part of a team came about serendipitously. At ten years of age, I was fortunate to have someone channel some of my erratic energy toward basketball.

One day after school, when I was in fifth grade at ICS, I was horsing around in the back of the auditorium with a few rough riders. We were kicking a ball against the doors of the gym, over and over again, and apparently disrupting the practice that was underway, being led by the coach. The coach was also my fifth grade teacher. One of my friends saw him approaching the doors and took off. A few of us remained, and when the doors opened, Coach Caporale grabbed me by the arm and told the others to leave immediately. He brought me into the gym while the members of the team were participating in drills. My brother Geoff, captain of the team, glared at me, which in translation meant, *"What did you do now?"*

In the coach's office, he told me to become part of the group and avoid foolish distractions. He said he wanted to include me in the team activities, to be part of a team, to feed the desire to learn and excel. I absorbed his words to my youthful capacity.

That point of intervention was an invaluable happening, and I became a member of the team. I enjoyed competing against the older players in practice, and this paid dividends over the three years to follow, until I became team captain in eighth grade. Leading and playing on a team allowed me to follow a tradition established by my three brothers just a few years prior. Playing on the basketball team in the fifth, sixth, seventh, and eighth grade helped me develop in a number of ways. As I earned more playing time over the years, I improved my skills, level of confidence, and performance. My understanding of the game progressed and so did my leadership capability. The real education came in my understanding the value of practice, teamwork, sacrifice, and effort, and how these factors impacted outcomes.

When I reached the eighth grade, my desire to compete accelerated, and the group of mentors I interfaced with widened. Beyond the ongoing internal feedback and direction I received from my brothers, Coaches

Caporale and Mongiovi and a new sideline motivator who entered the scene, Coach Dom Tana (aka Beepo), were available to provide constructive input. Tana was a friend to many in the neighborhood and enjoyed frequenting our games to provide insight and encouragement to the players. He also became the physical education teacher at ICS, which was kind of surprising, since he was running close to three spins on the scale at the time.

I first met Dom when I was fourteen. I was playing sports at the Gun Hill playground. Dom always enjoyed observing others compete. He loved his coaching and mentoring, and he seemed to be driven to build confidence in others by helping advance their skills. He would frequently say, "That's your best?" He would push us to compete more aggressively and would challenge or compliment us along the way. He was a special person.

Tana's primary employment was working in a group home just a few blocks from our school. As guardian and counselor to the troubled youth with whom he lived, he became very active in their education and after-school activities. One of the residents, Padro, played football with my brother Geoff and other standouts, like Cuomo (who also lived in the projects and was named High School All-American), at Evander Childs High School. Soon the nexus and diversity of friends rapidly expanded for me and my social group through involvement in sports and social interactions. Dom played a significant role in supporting and mentoring me and a wide swath of youngsters over the years. Legions of companions still enjoy his enthusiasm and guidance today. He is a neighborhood legend, chronic giver, and loving soul.

Another individual who was committed to offering his time and effort to supporting the development of our group was Tosi. He was a Bronx native, army veteran, and graduate of New York University, and he worked for the Bronx County NYC Board of Elections. He was an active participant in events held at the church and school and embraced the opportunity to serve as an ambassador for our basketball team. Tosi was a staunch advocate for serving the church and community in every way, most notably when Cardinal Edward Egan ordained him a deacon. He served at Immaculate Conception for many years and was involved in the youth ministry, sacramental preparations, and nursing home visitations. His wife of over half a century and scores of other parishioners found his presence comforting and spiritual.

A nucleus of community leaders and mentors emanated from our church. Programs to assist in the development of the youth outside of the framework of school included the Holy Name Society (HNS) and the Catholic Youth Organization (CYO). Both programs were designed to build character, integrity, and respect within its membership. I was pleased to be a member.

Jack was the central figure who started the HNS at ICS. He was eager to expand his existing association to include parish youth. Many of the standing members were church ushers and contributors who held meetings following services on Sunday mornings to address financial and parish-related matters. Jack wanted to broaden the program and attract a younger core to attend Sunday mass and participate in formal competitive sports programs on Wednesday evenings. In fact, the only way to become an active member and enjoy the sporting activities each week was to attend mass on Sunday mornings.

Over time, there was a surge in the number of youths who wanted to join in, but individuals would be turned away from participating if they were not enrolled on Sundays. You had to receive a membership card that could only be obtained by attendance on Sundays. "No Mass, No Card, No Gym"—this was posted on the auditorium doors, and identification was checked prior to entering on Wednesday nights.

Jack was serious in his efforts to teach us about the way of the streets and being smart in avoiding trouble. We had a diverse group of members from the projects and surrounding community. We heeded his advice and his attempts to establish resilience and strength in each of us. Jack would welcome each of us before the activities of the night commenced. As one of the youngest members, on most nights he would slap me softly on the face as a welcoming gesture. I would ask him, "What was that for?" He would reply, "Just in case you do something stupid." I would smile, walk away, and learn to avoid future greetings. We enjoyed the physical and emotional bond that formed within the group and appreciated everything Jack did to keep us in tune with the realities of the time.

The CYO assembly was younger than the HNS group. This core consisted primarily of high school–age youth. This team was diverse in every way, including males and females. These Tuesday-evening gatherings represented an extension of the parish services provided on Sunday, but they were toned down to allow freedom of expression in many forms. A couple of Capuchin Franciscan brothers were preparing to become priests and were the spiritual leaders who made every effort to provide a haven for learning, self-exploration, cohesion, activities, and cultural development. It was refreshing to see adolescents from the neighborhood socialize openly and discuss topics of the day.

At times, the brothers would prepare workshops to help stimulate discussions on various topics, allowing those who chose to participate to share their viewpoints and challenge others respectfully. We would occasionally take bus trips to the Jersey shore or attend Broadway plays. Yet the most memorable event coordinated was a play we created and carried out—a depiction of the Passion of Christ. The two budding priests directed many of the willing CYO participants. We held the enactment on Good Friday in the upper church for all parishioners.

The show was overwhelmingly appreciated by everyone who attended. Literally hundreds of family members from the parish embraced the rendition. Many weeks of preparation and practice led up to the performance. My brothers and I were excited to be part of the act. Geoff played Pontius Pilate, Gregory was an apostle, and I played a high priest. My future wife, Susan, played a weeping woman. She would learn years later that such a role was perfect for her considering my peculiarities. Gary was the designated photographer, capturing vivid impressions to last a lifetime. Seeing friends transform themselves into religious characters was refreshing. The reenactment of the Passion went on for a few years, until most of the actors aged, joined the workforce, or attended college. I have very warm memories of those special times, special friends, and developmental kinship.

There are too many wonderful memories to revisit, but the relationships formed at that time and, in a few instances, meaningful interactions and social dependence gave rise to long-standing, loving bonds that paved the way for marriage. At seventeen, I was one of the fortunate ones to meet my kindred spirit, confidant, and future wife, Susan, during our time at CYO. We enjoyed each other's company, laughed often, shared stories of family and friends, and prepared to embrace what the future offered.

The HNS and CYO were great banisters to help stabilize my transition from grammar school to high school in 1974. I attended Saint Raymond's High School for Boys in the East Tremont section of the Bronx. When I began as a freshman, I did not know any attending students, even though many were from different parts of the Bronx. I was fortunate, however, because early in the school year, basketball tryouts took place, and soon a promising team would take shape. I was privileged to make the freshman team, led by Coach Galilei, and was introduced to a collection of diverse students and teammates from regions outside of my familiar neighborhood.

A few months following the blending of our newly formed talent pool, we became champions of our division within the CHSAA league. With a record of 14–4, we were the most successful freshmen basketball team in Saint Ray's history. We were successful because we had our shepherd—an excellent coach who taught us to execute within a fundamental system operated by all basketball players at Saint Ray's. The system provided the framework, but our cohesion, commitment, and drive contributed to our success.

I was familiar with the varsity head coach, Piano, and junior varsity coach, Spears. Both were from the Bronx and lived in my neighborhood. They were contemporaries of my siblings and older friends, including Dom (Beepo), who played on the same team in various sports that they participated in. Soon, they became my teachers and coaches, and each played a key role in inspiring me to compete, achieve, and respect those I encountered each day. In the years following my graduation, we became close friends, sharing life events, and teammates, creating memories of competition in neighborhood softball leagues and pickup basketball games. They remain close friends today.

My four years at Saint Raymond's were a blessing. I had teachers who wanted to see everyone achieve high levels of performance. They were grounded and had our best interests in mind. The principal, faculty, and brothers focused our efforts on maintaining good grades and team spirit through discipline and effort. They readily encouraged participation in some sort of after-school activity. In retrospect, most of my friends who had a similar experience were very successful and went on to fine colleges and secured rewarding employment. I was pleased to become part of the National Honor Society at Saint Ray's and earned entry into Fordham University at the Rose Hill campus in the Bronx.

The discipline and structure provided was similar in scope to what I was accustomed to at Immaculate. Self-restraint and treating others with respect was a staunch expectation and one I came to learn when I stepped out of bounds. While it may have been an occasional event, it was not out of reach for a student to get a sudden backhand for being disrespectful to someone in authority, acting out, or disobeying rules.

Special discipline or being remanded after school for infractions committed were the common modes of discipline. On a couple of occasions, I was chastened. In most instances, at least in high school, it was because I was tardy to first period. I had to take two modes of public transportation to get to high school, and sometimes, with inclement weather, I was not in control. I should have tried out for the track team, as I had plenty of experience with running to catch a train or connecting bus. However, excuses or even logical explanations were not accepted, and I had to deal with the consequences, which I understood and accepted.

I did receive formal discipline in two instances. Back then, teachers in the schools I attended were not challenged for their methods of discipline. Even parents did not question teachers if the parents learned their child was disciplined for errant behavior.

When I was in grade school, I was removed from a class and offered a unique form of discipline. My teacher thought I was being disruptive and talking to students adjacent to me. I probably was, but the discipline didn't seem proportional to the infraction. The teacher informed my mother that I was "distracting" other students. When my mother told me of her conversation with my teacher, she said, "The discipline was warranted." I begged to differ but to no avail. I told her, "I really didn't do anything. Why are you not hearing what I have to say?" My mother just responded, "Stay out of trouble, and learn when to stop." I made a mental note and went on my way.

My second encounter with discipline was in high school, when a substitute teacher also thought I was being disruptive. This teacher was a true disciplinarian. When he filled in for one study class, he told us to be silent and read *The Book of Job* for the duration of the class.

After about thirty-five minutes into the forty-minute class, I grew bored and drew a beard on the front-cover picture of Job. I showed my artwork to my neighbor and teammate Charles, and we had a short-lived chuckle. Noticing the distraction, the teacher requested that I join him in front of the class and asked me if I was a quitter, to which I said no. At that instant, he felt inclined to discipline me for my behavior. The room grumbled with shock and dismay at what had happened, and the bell rang. I went back to my desk to retrieve my books, including the altered *Book* of *Job*, and walked out of the classroom. There was a buzz outside as classmates informed other students what had occurred. Mr. Spears (my teacher and coach) was leading the class next door, and when he learned of my violation, he went up to the teacher and asked what had happened. When informed, he told the sub that the incident was minor, and no discipline was required. The teacher sheepishly walked away in silence and most likely went back to his chamber to reflect and pray for the souls of those with swollen faces.

Those were my two encounters with school educators who felt inclined to discipline me. That's just two formal infractions in seventeen years. That's less than a 12 percent chance of being disciplined by a person in authority at school when having a lapse in judgment in almost two decades. So what did I learn? First, I came to understand the value of not being disruptive or disobedient. Second, I learned to avoid teachers with limited patience. To some extent, the discipline instilled fear, but to a greater extent, it instilled obedience and respect.

The interesting part of my grade-school encounter was the teacher's act of contrition many years later. The teacher contacted me and another restless classmate and invited us to lunch in the Morris Park section of the Bronx. This instructor had since left teaching and wanted to speak with us to see how we were progressing in our high school endeavors. Our discussion was pleasant. She told us that she was never really cut out for teaching and had become increasingly frustrated. This mentor also apologized for the distinctive form of discipline. We ate lunch, reminisced, and went on our way. I saw this former teacher one more time at a reunion. We spoke of aspirations and goals, and we wished each other well. I gave my former teacher a hug, which was my way of saying, *Thanks for the discipline.*

As for the substitute teacher, I never saw him again once I graduated high school, and that was okay with me. My prayers were definitely answered. I heard he opened a school of discipline for wayward students. No ... that's erroneous, and such a cavalier notation of his post school activities is simply foolish on my part. I deserve to be disciplined again for that one.

Sans the discipline, my experience at Saint Raymond's represented some of the most constructive years leading to college. I embrace today the solid friendships I formed. I cherish the attachments to the diversity of individuals who learned the same values of spirituality, commitment, independence, discipline, and drive and the expectation to achieve success. I am proud of the fact that there were never any issues of tension or violence between races within our school. We lived together for four years and grew into adulthood in harmony. I respect and appreciate the mentors and teachers who gave their time to help instill meaningful qualities in each of us. While today's forms of discipline for children are far too lax, with light consequences for poor behaviors, the discipline we received gave us the opportunity to learn and develop important competencies, including respect for others and keeping faith in our hearts forever.

CHAPTER 4

Educational Influence: All Children Can Learn

The Google dictionary defines *educational* as relating to the provision of education; intended or serving to educate or enlighten. *Influence* is the capacity to have an effect on the character, development, or behavior of someone or something, or the effect itself; a person or thing with the capacity or power to have an effect on someone or something.

Therefore, the Bronx educational influence I received during my foundational years of learning was intended to enlighten me and have an effect on or influence my character, development, and behavior. When we think of educational influence, we have a tendency to default toward our formal education in school. Again, we return to a prominent theme in this book that there is a wide band of influences that help guide us in the process of being educated. These influences are particularly important for children with learning disabilities.

The primary driver of states that mandate attendance to school is to build knowledge and to influence the behavior and character of its residents. In theory, having an educated, prideful, and civil society creates a culture that enables and propels individuals to achieve and capitalize on all available opportunities.

Like millions of others in the United States, I was directed to participate in the educational system. I had the option to attend public or private school or to be homeschooled. My parents chose to enroll their children in a private parochial school from kindergarten through eighth grade. Most of my friends within the projects attended public schools within the neighborhood, K–12. Some of their schools were in close proximity, and some required public transportation. An additional financial drain was placed on my parents for giving us a private education, but they believed that the structure and discipline was necessary and would align more effectively with the values and guidance they provided.

Following my siblings' graduation from grade school at Immaculate Conception, Nancy, Gregory, and Geoffrey attended public secondary school at Evander Childs High School, just a few blocks away from our apartment complex. My oldest brother, Gary, and I attended private high schools—Gary at Saint Francis Seminary in Newton, New Jersey, and I at Saint Raymond's in the Bronx, New York. Our education in parochial school and high school was not confined to the structure that each entity provided. The exchange of knowledge and information outside of school was pervasive in a variety of forums, each filled with data for us to absorb and interpret.

When you look at the composite schema of the available educational influences that impact and help shape our intellectual capacity, character, development, and behavioral tendencies, multiple attachments emerge. I can speak with the most authority about my own experience growing up. To that end, here is a simple list of the most important influences of my childhood. I use the term *influence* here to capture not just the people themselves but the key dynamics of my relationships with them that played a key role in my education. The knowledge gained from each of these learning vehicles is not arranged in any particular order, and I place no associated weight on any element:

- parental nurturing
- sibling alliance
- family extensions
- meaningful relationships
- pastors, priests, brothers, and leaders of the church
- grammar school, high school, and postsecondary institutions

- sports competition
- teachers, coaches, and school administrators
- employment experiences
- restaurant/tavern owners and customer base
- county political leaders
- local civil servants
- health care providers

This sorted list may not be all-inclusive, but it serves to illustrate how many touch points we have surrounding us and that, in one way or another, impact our thoughts, emotions, and aspirations.[16]

Depending upon my phase of development at a particular time and place, I may have gravitated more toward one element of learning than another. As example, when I was three or four years of age, with limited exposure to any formal schooling, I became attached to my parents and siblings for downloading information. This reality registered in different forms, from love and affection to guidance and discipline. Each educator provided his or her own version of what type of teaching should be provided, based upon their experiences.

My mother and father offered their unique brand, and my siblings contributed their individual interpretation and flavor of my parents' brand. As the youngest, my responsibility was to make an effort to assimilate, determine what was important to me, and understand how to react in certain situations. The good thing about having a variety of teachers at home early on was that when I did something wrong, I had the opportunity to course correct rapidly because they made me try, over and over again. Repetition was an important part of the learning

---

[16] I could prepare a chapter on each of the "educational influencers" referenced above, but that would detract from the primary focus of this guide. My intention is to present a simple yet targeted view of what is representative in every community and available for all individuals, regardless of race, religion, or creed. I will provide my best recollection of how some of these influential guardrails served to guide my decisions and to be in the best position to succeed in whatever life had to offer.

process, for me especially. To digest the information, I had to make an intense effort to replay scenarios again and again.

There were lots of distractions for me, and it was easy to get caught up in things that were outside of the framework of learning. As the youngest in the house, seeking attention was a form of interference for me. Everyone wanted to focus on their newfound learning opportunities and had little time to devote to my educational needs.

It takes some individuals longer to grasp concepts or instruction, particularly when underlying anxieties derail the progress of learning and development. I guess I fell into that category and was eager to explore new experiences beyond the confines of home. Entering grammar school in a new home at Immaculate Conception gave me that opportunity, but my learning uptake took time to kick into gear.

OUTSIDE AND IN

Kindergarten is the breakaway period for most children, a time of transition where the comfortable, secure structure they were afforded since birth with their parents is loosened.

During that separation, we were relegated to learning under a new umbrella of authority represented in the Catholic faith. The teachers were made up of nuns and tenured lay staff. For the most part, I enjoyed the environment and the support provided by the instructors. They were involved in all aspects of our development.

My first-grade teacher, Sister Claire, gave me fair to good ratings for traditional classes, and C's across the board for effort and B's for conduct. Based on the standards established by the school and their methods of evaluating performance, their assessment was that I was not fully separated emotionally from my parents and siblings, and my behavior and focus was inhibited. Additionally, having a narrow attention span and average grades at the onset, today I might have been labeled as having ADHD or auditory processing issues. This view seems like a plausible assumption, based upon my performance in the first couple of years, but in those days, we didn't yet have those diagnoses or terms.

Most parents paid particular attention to how their children progressed in reading, writing, math, and so on, but more important, they focused on the "Message to the Parents" on the back of the report card. This section defined both effort and conduct and commented on parental responsibility in the learning process. It seemed a much more thorough process than schools use today.

The rating for effort was based upon the following considerations (listed on my report card from first grade):

- Ability to concentrate; wise use of time; completion of work; steady attempts to improve; and participation in class discussions

The rating for conduct was described as:

- Respect for others; observance of regulations; polite attention when required; and care of property

The description of learning included, "You have begun the formation of your child's character. The school will help you to continue to teach good habits. Little will be achieved, however, unless you cooperate in every way that these habits be practiced outside the school, as well as within the school."

This was an interesting and direct communication to the parents, specifying their required follow-up to behavioral expectations. The synergistic relationship between the home and school environment, when working in unison, offered the best potential for yielding favorable outcomes for the student. At least this was the proposed objective, yet individual initiative was an overlying factor that impacted the results from one period to the next. This system was ideal for someone like me, but I attribute its success to the fact that parents had to work closely with the teacher to ensure follow-up to areas that required improvement of attention. Today, a child lacking both parents might not have the desired follow-up, and therefore, the behaviors or improvement noted might not receive the follow-up required.

As I progressed through the middle grades, I became more confident in both my schoolwork and after-school activities, such as sports. My supporting network, which included family, teachers, friends, coaches, priests, and mentors, grew wider and assisted me in improving my competence and behavior. My improvement on all fronts continued through graduation and carried through into high school at Saint Raymond's.

Heading into high school with a favorable wind of confidence was important. When I entered on my first day, I did not know any students that attended. This was not the case for long because early in my tenure at this new institution, I developed lasting friendships with classmates, teachers, teammates, and coaches.

Going to a Bronx high school that was not in my neighborhood was a blessing in disguise, and it helped me utilize my energy reserves most efficiently. Getting to school required an early wake-up and departure, using multiple forms of public transportation. First class started at 8:00 a.m., and the last concluded at 2:40 p.m. During the basketball season, practice would commence at three and go to five, and by the time I arrived home, it would be 6:30 or 7:00 p.m. I would eat something, start homework or study for an exam, and get ready for the next day. This became my routine for four years at Saint Ray's.

Along the way, I learned the importance of discipline, organization, and effort in maintaining excellent grades. Additionally, I was able to bolster my knowledge by learning the value of participating in team sports, and I recognized the commitment required to compete effectively and achieve positive results. I would draw upon these great life lessons in the years that followed. Leaving high school as a National Honor Society member gave me a heightened sense of capability and drive, which prepared me for attending Fordham University in the Bronx.

THE SCHOOL AT HOME

Pulsed within the traditional educational process were interstitial learnings that helped shape my thought process and decision-making. While experiential learning is important for all children, for a child with my particular issues, experiential learning was absolutely essential. As I became exposed to life-changing decisions that were made within my family, I learned in bounds. My loving siblings were guides and pioneers. By observing their behaviors and decisions, I came to understand the consequences for actions taken. A few examples surfaced with clarity pertaining to my siblings and their decisions to marry at a very young age.

My alternate caretaker and oldest sibling pressed her decision to marry shortly after graduating high school at just nineteen years of age. She was introduced to a US Marine through a friend, who also lived in the projects. I am sure she felt great joy and comfort, realizing that someone distinguished, who served in the US Armed Forces, gave her gratifying attention and affection. Coming from a larger family, she was inclined to liberate herself and explore the boundary of a newfound relationship with the intention of having her own family.

My mother and father tried feverishly to offer her guidance and counsel and expressed that her decision to wed was premature and erratic. My father was ardently against the wedding and the character of the individual she chose to be her soul mate. He was resolute in his defiance, and repelled all dialogue urging his participation in her plans. Nonetheless, my sister was headstrong and committed to proceed with her wedding. She was married at Immaculate Conception Church in January 1967. While I had no power in the situation, I saw that my sister was in an awkward position, and I felt bad for what she had to endure.

The strain between my sister and father eased over time. A couple of years after their wedding, my sister and her husband brought two boys into the world. I became an uncle at nine years of age, and suddenly, I felt much older. My father took great pride in seeing his grandsons when they came for visits from New Jersey. He loved to take them out for treats and parade them around for all to see. He did, however, grow weary of some of the behaviors of his son-in-law. Stress began to surface regularly between my sister and her spouse, which affected the behavior of my nephews. I observed the palpable tension firsthand when I stayed for weekend visits at my sister's. Frustration grew over their stalled landscaping business, and tensions continued to mount.

Over time, their relationship frayed, and the marriage dissolved. Trying to move to a higher plane, my sister made another unusual choice when she became linked to another unpredictable partner. She eventually settled with her children and new spouse in the Bronx, just a few blocks away from our home in the projects. She would add two more children in the mix, and her complications compounded as her new husband also wrestled with personal challenges. Years later, her second marriage would meet the same fate as the first. Subsequent relationships were fragile, and eventually, the cumulative stress from her fleeting relationships took its toll on her, mentally and physically. I always sympathized with her experiences, and her struggles even brought us closer to each other. As I grew up, despite her being older, I felt protective of her, though there's only so much one can do for another. She had to make her own decisions.

She suffered a debilitating stroke at age fifty, became nonambulatory with compromised speech, and remained under nursing home care for several years. She eventually joined my mother in the same nursing facility, until they both passed away in 2010. Mom died March 13 and my sister nine months later on Christmas Day. They were received with welcoming grace, and enjoy a peaceful spiritual happiness. My sister and mom were a significant source of inspiration. Even though they made tough decisions that may have negatively impacted their lives, they always supported and cared for me, no matter what. Their love and fiery characters are sorely missed, but their spirits remain.

My oldest brother has always been filled with the best intentions for himself and his family. He's good-hearted and always willing to help someone in need. His decision-making, however, was compromised. He too made a hasty miscalculation to marry prematurely. Upon his high school graduation from the seminary, he came to the realization that he was not going to be a priest. He was cemented in this belief because he engaged in a relationship with someone he met shortly after he graduated. His attachment grew stronger, even though his girlfriend was a few years younger and in high school. Following a brief experience in college, he was able to secure employment and kicked off his career in the telecommunications industry. His future bride soon graduated high school, and they continued to date. As his career began to take root and his relationship grew, he made plans for marriage.

At the same time, there was much communication from parents on both sides of the aisle, raising flags of caution over any potential nuptials, with which I agreed, even with my limited experience. Even though the couple appeared genuinely interested in pursuing marital bliss, family concerns over a lack of maturity and an understanding of relationships, were frequently offered as counter-proposals. Such suggestions were heard but did not register, and in the fall of 1976, my brother was married. Several years later, three children rounded out their family.

Raising a family was a joyous extension of his relationship, but over time marital challenges surfaced, and tensions persisted. Dissention and resentment inhibited any potential for a peaceful cohabitation. Eventually, they grew distant, separated, then made several attempts to reconcile, but ultimately, they terminated their marriage. Over time, their situation normalized, and all affected parties within the immediate and extended family acclimated to their new reality.

Recalling these troubling times of familial discord is not easy because the memories bring forward the pain and anguish that impacted the entire family at that time and place. There were tangible takeaways for learning through these troubling events, and in many respects, they strengthened family ties.

I learned the importance of drawing upon the experiences of parents, siblings, and others who provided valuable insight into designated plans. By watching my sister, especially, I learned the importance of cultivating a relationship over time. I learned the need to formulate plans that foster favorable outcomes. I learned that decisions made can have a significant impact on life experiences. I learned that it is okay to listen to those who are more experienced and have the best intentions for you. I learned that it's okay to care about others and seek to help them make difficult decisions.

More relevant: I recognized that anemic parental influence can have a debilitating and negative impact on the emotional maturity, decision-making, and development of children. I gained a general knowledge and understanding of the behaviors and interplay between individuals. I became more aware of the importance of education in the development of critical-thinking skills and the formulation of valuable solutions. I learned the important lesson of cultivating the construct of authentic loving relationships. Most important, I learned that maintaining faith and commitment to the teachings of the church is difficult, and we all need reinforcement through prayer and penance.

Another step on the educational ladder within the framework of the church was granted at Fordham University. I appreciated the religious instruction, social structure, and educational vigor the Bronx campus provided. I was pleased to earn the opportunity to attend. The transition from high school was seamless, as much of the orientation was similar.

As a premed student, I was exposed to a vast amount of information in the sciences but retained an insufficient amount to qualify for entry to med school in the United States. I opted to work while attending school, which was not a wise decision, considering the demands of the curriculum. Additionally, my commitment wavered, and my level of focus was erratic. In general, what I enjoyed most was the camaraderie, formation of friendships, and gaining an education in a great school. I graduated with a bachelor of science degree that prepared me to build a strong career in the health care industry. So, in retrospect, the tedious workload I endured paid significant dividends for my family and me.

Thinking about the specific decision to matriculate in the sciences as a premed student was an unrealistic objective. Weak self-awareness would apply in my case at that juncture. If I were to take a "mulligan," I might have selected a broad study in business and made an effort to play baseball for the Rams. Nevertheless, things do have a way of working out successfully if you play your hand right, use your God-given skills and talents to the fullest, and embrace sound leadership.

As the fifth and last child, I could not help but learn from those who came before me. Everything I had witnessed since birth provided portions of learning. Over time, I became aware of how bits of information are processed and subsequently initiated. I became sensitive to circumstances and determined if they felt right or not. I wanted to interpret what I observed, not simply follow what surrounded me. I preferred to lead, not follow.

Learning to interpret, retain, and recall information does not flow automatically for everyone, which is when experiential learning can be crucial, as it was in my case. This cerebral regulatory process varies for each individual, and in my case, the transmission of data was managed through interruptions. Put another way, at the cellular level of my brain activity, the neuronal connections and firings were not optimal. The pauses and interference in transmission from a given stimulus needed refinement, and the remedy came in the form of effort, time, and persistence. Those three elements are integral in the formula for learning.

Having the right mentors who care for you and want you to develop holistically makes all the difference in the world in all cases but especially in children with learning disabilities. Parents, siblings, teachers, coaches, friends, and other leaders responsible for your mental and physical well-being are all important contributors. Having those around you to inspire and motivate you early on is an important factor in building cerebral strength. Yet one of the most essential aspects of learning and development relates to individual effort and drive to achieve.

We all have the ability to learn. For some, the process is deliberate; for others, it may be accelerated. In either case, every community in the United States requires capable, caring, and patient educators, committed to assisting in the development of every individual they instruct.

CHAPTER 5

Personal Drive: Desire to Achieve

The definition of *drive* from *Merriam-Webster* is to carry on or through energetically; to compel to undergo or suffer a change; to impart a forward motion to by physical force.

Where does an individual's *drive* come from? For every person on earth, the answer to that question is nebulous. However, you can gain general insight by researching information related to personal drive and achieving success. The clinical data supported by psychologists reveals the longer an individual is committed to a task, the less important innate ability is, and the more important personal drive becomes. The most successful people across industries have just kept hammering away more consistently than others. The level of personal drive and motivation is proportional to personal growth and performance.

We are all driven for different reasons, and what propels us forward or keeps us in check or regressed depends on a variety of factors. What motivated me and many others to achieve consisted of a few converging elements. There were internal factors (e.g., skills, competitiveness, understanding, techniques) and external factors (e.g., praise, recognition, and approval) that prompted me to action to progress toward an established goal or objective. To be in a position to improve performance and outcomes, I had to push through and adjust when difficulties presented. I avoided negative thoughts and habits. I learned to pursue alternative approaches that helped me achieve my goals.

In reviewing information on the topic of personal drive, what I found fundamentally telling was revealed by a University of Chicago professor of education, Dr. Benjamin Bloom, and his work, *Developing Talent in Young People.*

He examined the critical factors that contribute to talent and success. What surfaces very clearly is that all the excellent performers he investigated had practiced intensively, had studied with devoted teachers, and had been actively supported by their families throughout their developing years.

> Simply put, parents who get the message across to their children (either by their own example or by explicit instruction) that being smart is better than not, that reading or active learning is better than watching television or wasting time, and that taking responsibility for certain tasks and for one's self is important, [those parents] produce children who are more able and eager to learn and consequently higher achievers.

> Parents who do not feel that learning is that important, or who for some reason are not able to get the message across to their children, tend to produce youngsters who have a harder time learning, presumably because they find it difficult to put in the effort required. ...[17]

> Over and over the [young people] made reference to the impact of teachers for whom they felt love, admiration and respect, and from whom they felt dedication to the field and to their students' development. Several said they were "going nowhere" when they worked with teachers who lacked such qualities.[18]

---

[17] Dr. Benjamin Bloom, *Developing Talent in Young People* (Random House, 1985), 141–142.

[18] Ibid., 499.

The educational system was established universally to develop young, malleable minds and instill personal drive to achieve through mentorship. The early years of childhood development are critical, as there is a narrow window to capture the attention of all those eager to learn. The duration for teaching and engaging the young in school is maintained, on average, for at least twelve years. That represents more than ample time to install the vital competencies required for all students to achieve. Having the right core of educators (working collaboratively with parents) with the drive and commitment to move individuals to a high plane of achievement can make a favorable difference in the performance and success of those they lead.

In similar fashion, the entertainment industry makes an effort to bring forward issues that can serve to inspire, motivate, stimulate thought, and move people. And most of the time, the intention is to drive people to take control of their circumstances. Unfortunately, it's a passive activity. What we see and hear from this industry is short-lived, disperses over time, and has limited effect on driving individuals to achieve. That's not the case with the standards established within our educational system. In my own life and in my observations, classrooms and life experiences have the most impact over time.

For example, there is a very crude but telling scene in the 1976 movie *Rocky*, where he is trying to caution a neighborhood teen, Marie, against associating with the wrong people. He makes an attempt to offer insight on the formation of personal character through the eyes of others. He advises her to avoid those who have little personal drive or self-esteem. He tells Marie very directly, "You hang out with nice people, you get nice friends, ya understand? You hang out with smart people, you get smart friends. You hang out with yo-yos, you get yo-yo friends. You see, simple mathematics." And Marie callously responds, "Screw you, creepo!"

Sometimes, we can provide advice and suggestions in order to help steer the young in the right direction, but that does not mean that the recommendations will be observed. Regardless of the actions taken by our youth, educators need to be intensely vigilant of the level of effort and drive their students put forward.

For most of us living within the projects, a personal drive emanated from our wanting to achieve more. There was a competitive element, borne of the early competition in sports, and an inspirational component that resulted from not wanting to relive hardships experienced during childhood. Most of us began to formulate career goals once we progressed through high school. We may not have had a definitive path selected, but the thought process started to percolate as we approached adulthood.

As I have previously discussed, engaging in team sports became an active method for channeling energy, enhancing mental clarity, and improving performance. In my middle-school years, I became increasingly driven to compete and improve my skills. I was eager to participate in sports activities with older players in school and the neighborhood. I wanted to surpass their capabilities outright. Taking this approach bolstered my talent and yielded greater self-confidence and willingness to set higher goals.

Understanding the process of skill development, through patience and practice, deepened my commitment and drive. Eventually, it became irrelevant to know who my competitor was, and all that mattered was performing at the highest level possible. Ultimately, as my skills and talents progressed, favorable outcomes followed. Developing confidence by way of engaging in sports competition had a meaningful carryover effect in school and in my association with family and friends. Additionally, this newfound self-assurance would serve me well in the years ahead at college and when entering the workplace.

I soon became eager to learn every nuance of a sport. Unconsciously, I was building confidence by learning how to improve. Without my knowing it, I was building in myself greater competence and leadership. This enthusiasm and initiative would again be revealed with each employment opportunity. My objective was to become well versed in the expectations outlined and to maintain a high level of competitive drive to achieve the highest level of performance. On occasion, I fell short of my objectives. In those instances, I became driven to learn new methods to improve my effectiveness and find solutions to achieve positive results.

In the personal-drive development process, involvement in team sports represented one side of the equation. The other side, as I mentioned above, signified a confidence element that led to greater focus in school and an early projection for establishing a career. Growing in confidence through sports and work served as an important motivator. The drive to achieve and produce excellent results became a constant driver.

Being driven was important because I wanted my parents, family, and friends to recognize my accomplishments. I was prideful and committed to doing whatever I had to do in order to achieve. My parents, siblings, and friends put more than enough energy into my development, and my being able to achieve established goals was a rewarding way of giving back. I wanted them to embrace any success I experienced in my years of education and employment. My parents sacrificed more than most would have, and any modicum of success for each of their children brought them great joy.

We were driven by the elements that everyone is driven by, but the love and union of our environment brought these elements to life:

- personal values and leadership
- competition and success
- recognition and approval

PERSONAL VALUES AND LEADERSHIP

As referenced earlier, the fundamental truth that we all understood and embraced within the projects was to lead our lives in a respectful, humble manner. Our parents expected it, and they held us accountable to it. We were to demonstrate self-respect and to respect others, regardless of contrasts. We learned to treat others with compassion and understanding because they were experiencing the same realities as we were. We were constantly reminded to have the courage to stand for what is right and to gain the respect of those around us.

Living with such childhood expectations gave rise to an understanding of the essence of leadership. Together, we learned what it means to be a leader. I understood that, as a person in charge, I had to establish expectations, values, and principles to which I was willing to hold myself and my group. Building an understanding of leadership early on helped me earn the respect of others rapidly. Such learning helped me form trusted alliances throughout my tenure in school and in the workplace.

Learning to network and associate with the right people—those who shared a common core of values—helped place me on trajectory to advance and ultimately lead at a high level. My progression toward any degree of success as a leader within the organizations I was part of was clearly attributed to the standards established and adhered to. Any formulation of strategies, tactics, and execution plans was rooted in a transparent belief system. Having a platform of ideals, which everyone within the organization was committed to implementing, was central to achieving success.

COMPETITION AND SUCCESS

Competition motivates all of us to do our best. Living in a housing project meant someone else was in very close proximity to you and in a similar social sphere. To have someone living in the immediate vicinity made for an ideal competitive environment. All of us were very competitive—you just had to watch a Saturday afternoon basketball game at Gun Hill playground to see how competitive we were. My brothers, Gary, Greg, and Geoff, would get after it pretty good when competing. Greg was interesting to observe. He always maintained a calm, reserved demeanor; he is one of the nicest people you could meet on the planet. Yet when he engaged in sports, he morphed into a driven demon, a real competitive lion. Sparks ignited, and tempers flared often, but what really mattered was who won. This was the reality in any sporting event in our neighborhood. Realizing that someone was better than you was a powerful source of motivation.

The reality of such a dynamic within our living space was not really shocking, as it followed the behavioral path that had existed since the beginning of time. The human species evolved with an automated mapping toward competition, particularly when individuals are confined to the same territory. Survival of the fittest, in all its fervor, is what kept us strong and active. To know that the neighbor you lived with from as far back as you can remember was performing better than you was a powerful and steady motivator for achievement. And over time, such a competitive drive served many in the neighborhood well, as most progressed and built solid careers across various industries.

However, staying motivated, driven, and focused in such a competitive environment was difficult. We progressed through each day with all its happenings, and not everything remained in equilibrium. It would have been great if the arena we operated within remained at a steady state while we pursued our goals. But the reality of life brought speed bumps and roadblocks that we had to learn to navigate.

Being someone who was easily distracted, it was not uncommon for me to get derailed from any of the many established goals or objectives. What I required in order to achieve and succeed was a steady diet of motivation. And the most powerful sources of motivation, for me, were my parents, siblings, other family members, and friends who experienced similar life disruptions and stayed the course. I listened carefully to those who were successful, and I tried to understand what made them effective. I learned to surround myself with people I could draw from. I made a habit of asking lots of questions and requested suggestions on how to approach a given task. I learned the value of being resourceful, finding solutions to challenges, and incorporating methods to place me in the best position to achieve success.

Knowing that family and close friends had to compete relentlessly and remain steadfast in their drive to achieve prompted me to do the same—and more. There is special behavioral psychology about seeing close friends achieve success. From my perspective, it instills a belief that if they were able to achieve, then I could as well.

RECOGNITION AND APPROVAL

It is widely accepted that we all want and need to be recognized and valued. Every human requires affirmation that others accept their energies, contributions, and interactions as meaningful. In the absence of such recognition, individual drive and commitment may dissipate, leading to reduced involvement and performance. Many times, people fail to provide others with recognition because it requires additional time and effort, or they think it is unnecessary. Some believe that by constantly recognizing positive behaviors in individuals, you run the risk of weakening their drive to achieve. Yet those with that particular mind-set often desire praise and recognition. Individuals who are quick to receive praise but hesitate to offer it are usually weak leaders or mentors, and over time, they lose the respect and trust of those they are charged to inspire.

"As children we constantly seek praise and approval from our parents and other adults ("Mummy, Daddy, look at me!"). The yearning for praise and recognition is a survival mechanism and is ingrained in us from such a young age that one could argue that it is very difficult to let go of it as adults."[19] From the time we were born, we desired and required recognition and approval.

The young primarily seek approval from their parents and extended family. Human beings are hard-wired with a survival code that is activated once they leave the mother's womb. In a similar way, once the recognition gene is triggered in the brain, there is no turning it off. There is a constant longing for approval and validation for actions taken. And the actions taken or behaviors displayed are relative to what parents have programmed and what is seen and heard. The

---

[19] resurgenceblog.wordpress.com/2012/11/11/seeking-recognition-and-approval-are-we-looking-in-the-right-places.

approval trait is transmitted to all of us, and we broadcast it to all those we encounter.

The drive for recognition and approval is inherent in every human, and no one can escape its force and influence. Who doesn't seek the approval of others? I know I did. As far back as I can remember, I always had a propensity to be recognized. Was it because I was the youngest of the clan? Perhaps that is part of the equation. And when you overlay a genetic expression with the reality of being the last of a tribe, you get a ferocious requirement to be heard and seen.

The good news for all of us living in the projects was that we could not avoid being recognized for our actions. Sometimes, the actions taken were received favorably and other times not so satisfactorily. Someone was always available within or outside of the home to provide interpretations of our behaviors. Either way, we were recognized and received the corresponding feedback.

What we learned was that recognition and approval for doing things right was the preferred form of acceptance. If we did something right, we wanted the stamp of approval from others, yet over time, that requirement waned. As we became more secure and confident, we didn't necessarily seek the recognition of others. In contrast, we became more aware that by doing the right thing, we were pleasing and recognizing ourselves, and we did not require the approval of others. This was an invaluable lesson that helped me and many others understand the importance of trusting ourselves and actions taken.

It's ever so important that children have the proper discipline while they're young, in elementary school and above, so that confidence—so necessary for life—is cultivated in them. Once we reach adulthood, we're expected to know how to be successful and my siblings and I received that cultivation. Children today don't get it in the same volume or consistency. Educators could learn a lot from those of us who grew up in a time when discipline was more rigid and experiential learning was encouraged.

CHAPTER 6

Loving Relationships: Sharing Love and Joy

*M*errriam-Webster* defines *relationship* as the fact or state of having something in common and the state of having shared interests or efforts; the way in which two or more people or things are connected, or the state of being connected.

The fact or state of having something in common cannot get more intense than the connection between parents and their offspring. The kinship created is a divine assembly of thoughts and emotions that supersede any association with others. The linkage and formation of common interests is built upon the foundation of love and admiration. We all have a strong desire to fit in and be part of a tribal unit. The bond of parental love is the framework that gives meaning to all that we do.

Our parents represent the foundation of our association and affinity for understanding and experiencing loving bonds with others. Without the reflection and orientation of love from our parents, we would be challenged to give love to another outside of the family unit. All children long for and require parental love. Parents are inherently capable of giving children all the love they need. We all carry an evolutionary gene that triggers a natural instinct to nurture and protect, particularly mothers.

Research has shown that authentic parental love helps the child's brain grow faster than that of a neglected child. The parental nurturing received helps stimulate growth of the region in the brain responsible for learning and memory, and such early growth can have a prolonged effect on development during childhood. So as parents, if we want to raise happy, well-adjusted, confident children who grow to become caring, learned adults, we have to make every effort to avoid or limit environmental infiltrations and to do what comes naturally.

A 2015 study from the University of Notre Dame reveals that "children who received affection from their parents were happier as adults. Those who reported less affection struggled with mental health, tended to be uncomfortable in social situations, and were less capable of relating to others."[20]

Having an intact nuclear family was a precious reality growing up in the Gun Hill projects. In fact, most of the greater than one thousand children contained within our Bronx housing association had the good fortune of being bolstered by two parents living in the same household. Based on my observations, in the '60s and '70s, having a traditional parental base was rather commonplace and served to curtail or repel any negative external forces that presented within our community.

From the time we entered the world and received a tap on our bottoms, expelling any maternal fluids, we were destined to form a powerful and unbreakable bond with our mothers. From that period on, the ability to form durable relationships depended upon the early experiences with the caregivers who consistently met our needs for sustenance, protection, and social stimulation. For the most part, our mothers provided the nurturing, and our fathers provided the structure and defined boundaries in the development process.

AFTER THE WOMB

After my birth, my mom was separated from me because she hemorrhaged following my delivery. Her life was in jeopardy as a result of my arrival. For a few weeks, I was left in the care of my father, sister,

---

[20] https://psychcentral.com/news/2015/12/23/parents-touch-support-play-vital-to-kids-happiness-as-adults/96613.html.

and extended family members, who provided me with the necessary nourishment to grow and helped me to become sensitized to my new environment. That brief period of division was just enough separation to make me that much more desirous for parental security. While that may be somewhat of a stretch, it's hard to imagine how a child can endure the offerings of environmental instability in the absence parental engagement. My mom did recover and regained her function well enough to support my early development. We all need a parental blanket to keep us healthy. And I appreciated the warmth and comfort my parents and siblings provided me from birth to adulthood.

Despite the initial separation, the loving bond formed with my parents since birth was a formative precursor to establishing loving relationships with my siblings, extended family, and friends within my community. Forming friends was not that difficult in the projects. There was much similarity—our two-parent households, especially—that linked us together, even through the prism of diversity. It is precisely because of the parental nurturing and guidance we received that we were able to form meaningful friendships, adapt to environmental stress, and maintain mental health with the capacity to learn.

As referenced in previous chapters, distractions did impact our family, but there was never any diminution of care to cause a fractured unit. The immediate extension of the loving union with my parents was the mutual devotion of my siblings. While their personalities were remarkably unique, each one of my beloved siblings was similar in their willingness to accept, encourage, protect, guide, and love me. Despite their busy schedules, they always tried to make time for me.

We did everything together when we were younger. At least I was eager to cling to their bootstraps, while they willingly welcomed my desire to engage. We played, ate, challenged, learned, and shared our faith together. We helped each other in need and took responsibility for our actions. When disciplined, we tried to comfort each other and chalked it up to a new learning experience. My childhood education with my family was a wholesome and valued time and one that helped prepare me to embrace any event to follow.

Our family friendships within the projects and surrounding community were numerous, binding, and enduring. We got to know them intimately and took an interest in their daily activities, relationships, and circumstances. We all lived in the same confines and learned to play well in the sandbox. Most of our immediate building neighbors became friends to lean on, and we enjoyed each other's company. We had family gatherings on occasion in our apartments, where adults and children would share food, stories, laughter, and life's happenings. All the families had personal challenges to overcome. The family gatherings helped provide a brief respite from any obstacles that a family member may have experienced. And of course, there were arguments and heated debates on how to address situations or general viewpoints on family matters, but these debates only brought us closer. And we continued to grow together in harmony as we aged through adulthood. Eventually, neighbors moved, traveled to college, went off to war, married, died, started careers, or remained intact in the same confines and made new friends. In any case, the early friendships formed and remain solid and are cherished today.

I hesitate to provide examples of the wonderful, loving relationships formed because the families involved are numerous, and if I were to omit any one family, I would be ostracized or banished to Bogeyland. But I'll take my chances with one of our direct neighbors. The Hirt family lived right next door in apartment 4H, across the hall, five feet from ours. My mom and Irene became great friends, and our families spent an inordinate amount of time together. Irene lost her husband when her children were young. Their father was a New York City police officer who served bravely and, unfortunately, died in the prime of his life after battling Hodgkin's lymphoma.

My family built a solid relationship with the Hirts and enjoyed their company in every way, every single day. They were genuine neighbors. My brothers and I shared many years of competitive sports, playing in various leagues with the Hirt brothers. Fred was more controlled in his efforts, but Randy had a tendency to become unhinged at times, to his detriment. We belonged to the same circle of friends from the neighborhood and enjoyed many years of pleasantries. Fred went on to attend Manhattan College and later entered the exciting field of computer technology. Randy and my older brother Gary were eager to join the workforce and applied at the Western Electric plant in Tuckahoe, New York, when they were young adults. They secured jobs and worked together for many years, as they both built solid careers that lasted decades in the telecom industry.

Loneliness was an issue for our neighbor when the father died. It was immensely difficult for the Hirt family to endure, but we were able to help them heal and became an extension of their family. Over the years our families remained cohesive, and we preserved our relationship. And as time progressed, following our journey in the projects, our parents aged and passed on gracefully. But the loving memories we created then blend seamlessly into the new ones that unfold today with our expanded families. We cling to the bonds formed many years ago, and we embrace a relationship that will endure.

Friendships formed in the neighborhood and schools came together easily. We were all eager to enjoy the company of those around us. We embraced our camaraderie each day, and we were very protective of the relationship that bound us together. If there was any attempt from outsiders to invade our space and disrupt our bond, they were met with staunch resistance. This reality became very apparent when competing in sports leagues across the city.

Within each league, players from different neighborhoods competed for a championship, and such aggressive competition gave rise to heated challenges. If you were going to stake your claim at the top of the heap, you would have to earn it. If a player on your team was confronted forcefully, many teammates were ready and willing to intervene rapidly. Such an alliance created everlasting bonds of trust and respect. This type of allegiance carried over in many aspects of our lives. The protection of firm relationships carried over in school, in the workplace, and within community activities. Our strength in team unity built resilience and confidence in each of us.

When we were not engaged at home, in school, or competing in sports, it was commonplace to just hang out on the street, discussing the topics of the day, which might have included how our favorite sports team was doing, school events, family happenings, work and finances, news reports, or spats between neighbors. As we got older, we followed the same pattern, but instead of hanging out on the streets, we congregated in gyms, ball fields, and local taverns. That was a common progression in our neighborhood and a method of preserving the bonds of friendship and belonging.

This new setting offered an even broader extension of friendships by way of an older generation willing to provide wisdom through experience. In any one gin mill within our Bronx locality, you would find several generations of people, communicating, connecting, and sharing stories of common interests. The intergenerational relationships formed were meaningful, enjoyable, and lasting. And while some of those Bronx locations closed, many of the same people migrated to alternate establishments to continue the rich heritage of sharing good will, laughter, and firm ties of friendship.

My brother Geoff worked at a local tavern and grill for years while going to college. He was determined to become owner of that same business we all frequented, and he eventually did just that, establishing the Four G's Tavern and Restaurant in 1991. He was able to help preserve the foundation of great relationships, and we all have great and lasting memories. He maintained that retreat of learning and unity for twenty years until other family and employment priorities required his time and efforts. He was proud to be able to preserve the integrity of our union. We are forever grateful for his love and are proud of him for his generosity and spirit of giving.

Still today, we preserve our long history and routine in other friendly locales, such as the world-renowned River's Edge, owned by longtime cherished Bronx neighbors and dear friends Dom and Rocco. There, relationships formed over half a century ago are maintained, and new bonds of friendship continue to blossom.

Additionally, I tend to frequent other portals in the Bronx and Westchester, where I have formed an even wider circle of friends, sharing common relationships—places like Bridges, owned by a driven, successful entrepreneur and loyal comrade, Brook, where many former high school mates and Bronx residents find solace from life's pressures. I enjoy friendly havens that serve up good food, good vibes, and good times, including Enzo's of Arthur Avenue, Pasquale's Rigoletto, and Antonio's, right in the heart of the Bronx Little Italy, adjacent to Fordham University. In Westchester, there are similar shelters, like Chatterbox 54 and B&Bs. In each location, I remain comfortable and am reminded of the great people of the Bronx and the ties of friendship and respect.

Loving relationships formed in the Bronx grew into meaningful long-lasting bonds. One of the most important connections that I made as a teenager was the loving, kindred alliance that has flourished over the past four decades with my wife, Susan. As teenagers, we develop many friendships, yet not every relationship grows into a wholesome, gratifying experience. I was fortunate to align myself with a loving, selfless, spiritual soul. Even though we knew of each other in grammar school at ICS, I gained progressive interest in building a relationship with her the more I was around her during early adulthood. I was attracted to her in every way. She presented a genuine interest in others. Our families shared similar values and viewpoints on life matters. She loved to laugh, and we learned that by sharing joy and laughter, we could shield ourselves from any negative influences. We connected; we were eager to build a lasting relationship, and we did. We married in 1989, and we are blessed to have three beautiful, loving children: Daniel, Amy, and Emily. Our family is as integrated as you can get, and we respect and enjoy each other's thoughts, emotions, and differences. We are bound by love and respect for each other, our family, and faith. I embrace every experience we have had to date, and I look forward to new revelations that we encounter each day.

I learned—through observations from within my family and those in the community—that building a loving and meaningful relationship with a soul mate is a special, rare experience. Each of us can form such relationships by being more aware of the underlying drivers that construct firm unions. My take on the foundation of developing a pure, loving, and lasting union is rooted in the core values of this book[21]

---

[21] Respect for self and others, a desire to achieve goals, and taking pride in oneself.

and in the synergy of the three C's ... where one blends favorably and seamlessly into the other:

- compatibility
- communication
- compromise

The first and perhaps most important cornerstone is *compatibility*. A primal nature has tentacles throughout the evolutionary process. We all possess a deep-rooted drive and desire for what we deem attractive. We long for the opportunity to be united in every way ... physically, mentally, and spiritually. When you hear people say, "It was love at first sight," that's not really accurate. They may have developed a loving relationship over time, but the first sight and thoughts were driven by raw desire and loving intentions—that's physical attraction. To suppress that as reality is to erase millennia of tribal desires and emotions geared toward the opposite sex.

Once you come to learn that you are definitely compatible, you can move to a higher ground and overlay mental and spiritual unification. Having a firm base of physical attraction, coupled with a shared value system of beliefs, helps cement firm ground to build your relationship. Try to bridge to the next building block—*communication*—in the absence of compatibility and you will run into some challenges.

Merriam-Webster defines *communication* as "the act or process of using words, sounds, signs, or behaviors to express or exchange information or to express your ideas, thoughts, feelings, etc., to someone else."

I posit that it is very difficult to freely express behaviors, thoughts, ideas, and feelings to a desired partner in the absence of a developed compatible bond. In fact, we know that when relationships erode, the first element to vacate and take center stage is communication. "We don't communicate anymore" or "We don't communicate like we used to" are common pleas of those losing a grip on their once-solid relationship. Compatibility leads to unfiltered, genuine

communication, and when these elements are th.
are more apt to want to compromise.

My good friends at *Merriam-Webster* share the de.
compromise as "a settlement of differences by arbitration or by c.
reached by mutual concession." I say it's a way to mend the bas.
differences that exist between a man and woman. Trying to remember
that it's not all about you is a great reminder and adage to help preserve
any relationship, let alone one that is intended to last a lifetime. Building
a solid relationship requires much give-and-take from each partner.

Men and woman are physiologically and psychologically different.
The differences in appearance and physical stature are obvious. There
are differences in how each shares emotion, differences in hormonal
chemistry, differences in how they react to stimuli, and differences
in how they connect to each other. Simply put, men and women are
just very different. So how can you build a long-lasting union with a
partner who is very different from you? Well, based upon the current
rate of divorce, flip a coin, and you will have the same chance of
figuring out those issues. However, in reality, if you take the time to
cultivate a relationship and remain conscious of the cornerstones that
help support a meaningful partnership, you will be in the best position
to make the right decision.

Why the breakdown in relationships? What gets in the way? What
environmental or cultural factors creep in? There are myriad reasons
why we see tarnished and eventually damaged relationships that
result in single parents. As referenced earlier, marital dissolution is
still very prevalent in our society, so it seems logical that spending
time developing a holistic relationship before leaping into marriage
can help your partnership endure the test of time. Much of how we
react to pressures or outside influences we learned from our parents,
personal observations, and experiences. Capably dealing with anxiety,
as well as other igniting factors, can have a tangible impact on how we
maintain relationships.

There is no doubt that having two parents and extended family
to draw upon during childhood provides a series of learning and
educational experiences that prepares you to navigate through life

..nallenges and capitalize on opportunities to help you achieve. There are more than enough data in archives that support the favorable impact on children's development in having two parents living with their children.

I want to be clear about any reference to nuclear, intact, or traditional families. As I stated earlier, my intention in the guide is to provide an overview of reasonable, sound building blocks that can assist individuals in building strength in the young they lead.

I recognize that in 2018, the percentage of nuclear families, as compared to the '60s and '70s, is dramatically lower. My point of orientation is not intended to stereotype or disparage families of today that may take on varying nontraditional forms. Leading the young through a diverse framework can yield favorable outcomes. The challenges to overcome are amplified, yet children can still progress when both parents are committed and intimately involved. I will, however, draw corollaries to the nuclear families from the era of my childhood and their impact on the health and outcomes of those who were nurtured under such practices. We can all do in-depth research on the inherent value of nuclear or traditional families and some of the trials that present to nontraditional families, and we can gain intellectual insight of the relative value under either scenario.

Collins English Dictionary defines a nuclear family as "a family unit that consists of a father, mother, and children." Wikipedia, the free encyclopedia, under the "Usage of the term" section (extracted from the *Merriam-Webster Dictionary*), highlights the nuclear family as "a household consisting of a father, a mother, and their children all in one household dwelling."

As referenced, the context of this manual is to give my perspective and logic on building strength in the youth of America. It is clear to me that a child growing up in a nuclear family in the twenty-first century will be more apt to develop the skills, self-confidence, emotional stability, mental clarity, and social readiness to achieve success. As noted, fundamentally, not much has changed in our society, as compared to the society of the '60s and '70s. In fact, if we have changed, we have made some considerable reversions, as it relates to the development of the young in our country.

What have changed are the self-imposed standards of immediate gratification and self-centered generational norms. Cultural distractions have eroded the family unit and created a wedge between parenting and childhood development.[22] As a result, the formation and continuity of loving relationships from generation to generation is compromised. Many of the young across our country are not mentally prepared to learn and acquire the skills necessary to compete and succeed in their endeavors.

Consider the billions of dollars budgeted for education each year within our communities, and evaluate the outcomes for childhood readiness to achieve. The results are not satisfactory. As an example, New York City, in the past five years, spent approximately $121 billion purely on educational operating expenses. The outcomes of the associated costs and the effort put forward reflect a graduation and college readiness rate well below the state and national norms, at 85 percent.

We know the percentage of children raised under a nuclear family within the New York City educational system is relatively low. According to the 2017 County Health Ranking Report, on average, "41% of children are living in single-parent households within the five boroughs of NYC, ranging from 28% to 62%."[23] Therefore, we can make a logical assumption that by increasing the focus on maintaining the integrity of the family unit, we can expect improved educational outcomes. And this proves to be true when you look at public high schools within New York City in communities with intact families; the rates of graduation surpass the city average of 68.1 percent (as calculated by the NYS method). As example, the 2017 NYC Department of Education report reflects the "four-year graduation rate for students

---

[22] The data regarding the rate of divorce from the '70s to the present decade show dramatic increases. And as the rate of divorce increases, so does the impact on the development of children in America.

[23] www.countyhealthrankings.org/app/new-york/2017/measure/factors/82/data?sort=desc-0.

within the Bronx at 63%." The Bronx also has the highest percentage of children living in single-parent households, at 62 percent. Conversely, students in "Staten Island have a graduation rate of 79.1%" with 28 percent of children in single-parent homes.

The distinction here is meaningful, considering there are 1.1 million students in the NYC school system, which represents the largest school district in the United States.

Yet each year within each state and municipality, we continue to fund traditional educational programs[24] and hope for a recognizable change in improved outcomes. It seems more practical to allocate a portion of community educational funds toward early childhood learning. Create a platform that centers on the preservation of the family unit and its impact on childhood development, learning, and achieving improved performance. More specifically, we need to create a learning program that addresses the need for parental supervision and support in the learning process, where two parents are actively engaged. The Department of Education also needs to provide additional resources, where needed, to bolster childhood learning.

Preserving the integrity and value of the nuclear family by keeping the family intact is an essential element for effectively developing our youth and teaching them the fundamental aspect of forming loving relationships.

---

[24] Includes the daily routine of children attending class and participating in core requirements, with limited or no involvement in additional support programs.

CHAPTER 7

Organization and the Workplace

M*erriam-Webster* defines *organization* as "the act of or process of organizing or being organized. Systematize; to arrange one's things or affairs so they can be dealt with effectively." From my perspective, being consistently organized means maintaining order and being free of distractions or clutter. Maintaining your surroundings in a simple and clear fashion curtails overstimulation of brain cells and keeps your mind and body in homeostasis.

The Chinese utilize an abstract system known as feng shui to create balance between individuals and their environment. The words feng shui, meaning "wind and water," represent a real-world approach to using our surroundings to attract positive energy into everything we do. Most people who capture our attention favorably and give off a "positive vibe" are capable of harnessing an unobstructed flow of energy and using it to create peace of mind.

During childhood, I learned that it was easier and more advantageous to live each day within peaceful, organized confines. I think this type of living arrangement would benefit everyone. Living within a compressed housing complex and apartment as the youngest of a large family brought forward more than enough stimulation and brain activity. There was always something going on, something to do, or something to accomplish—always. Finding opportunities to decompress, channel emotions, and clear my mind came about by developing organizational skills. However, advancing these skills took practice.

Any reference to organizational skills in this chapter refers to the state of being organized, as outlined in the definition above—I don't want to insert confusion by drawing any correlation to organizational habits that relate to administrative or managerial capabilities. However, the two depictions do intersect in the workplace, and both are important elements for achieving successful outcomes.

Today, some believe I have a very active mind or maintain a divergent thought process—ADHD, perhaps. Although I've never been clinically diagnosed with attention deficit hyperactivity disorder, my wife has confirmed the diagnosis. As she often says, "There is no doubt in my mind whatsoever." If that's the case, then so be it. Over the years, I have tried to adapt and curb this "assigned condition" by learning to plan and organize my thoughts and actions. Balancing or streamlining thoughts can be an effective way of softening the effects of the stress we store each day.

Growing up in a housing project, surrounded by literally hundreds of families and living with six other family members in a three-bedroom apartment, easily created an environment where things tended to accumulate. Whether it was clothes, furniture, dishes, or daily chores, something would build up. At school, a similar scene would unfold. We had to be on time, line up when the bell rang, head to homeroom, gather books, head to class, and go to recess. Classes would resume, then lunch, recess, and classes continued until dismissal. We prepared for after-school activities, headed home, had dinner, did homework, played games or watched TV, prepared for next day, and went to sleep. This was the same daily routine for each of us, over and over. Therefore, we had no choice but to foster an organized arena for living and learning.

Now imagine these scenarios outlined in the absence of a normal state of organization and planning. Lots of things would gather, and there would be more than enough stimulation available for everyone. Stress would emerge and become potentially burdensome. Excessive stressors can wreak havoc over time and take their toll on our mental and physical health. So it behooves all of us to learn how to live life in an organized manner. Think about the favorable effects and benefits of having all people within our communities living peacefully, more controlled, and less stressed. Organizational synergy can bring about peace and harmony in highly populated environments.

My parents were different in how they carried out their daily functions, and their different style allowed me to develop my own habits, based on what I observed and what suited my needs.

My father was extremely particular. He was proud of his attention to detail, accuracy, and organization. He conducted his business in a very orderly fashion and expected everyone else to do the same. This was the same expectation he had for his siblings' decades earlier and one that manifested vibrantly with his children. He worked hard, rested, ate, demanded order, and worked some more.

My mother had an alternate approach. She was a true workhorse. Even though we would all have chores to do and pitch in where we could, my mom would try to do just about everything. She worked, shopped, cooked, cleaned, did the laundry, and expressed her thoughts and emotions freely, and she made every effort to tend to our individual needs. Very rarely did my mother have any downtime; she was always on the go. Stress would inevitably seep in, and she would display signs of frustration from time to time.

We were not the most proactive group in tending to our responsibilities, and as a result, things would gather. The accumulation of things, activities, or events would have a pronounced effect on her overall health and well-being. She was a doer and giver. Unfortunately, she wanted to do too much and pushed herself to the limit, giving too much of herself to too many. She not only maintained the foundation of her home, but she was also called on to help care for her nieces and nephews when her sons were working or not available. She spread herself out too much, and it eventually took its toll on her, mentally and physically.

We learn plenty from our environment and our ability to absorb information. We learn from what we see and hear each day. How we choose to organize our lives is a reflection of what we were accustomed to during our childhoods. Those of us who grew up in loving, two-parent households had strong, present role models, so we manage our affairs, in some respects, the way our parents did, and we adopt our unique stance on being organized. The blended approach allows us to navigate and teach accordingly. Sometimes the path chosen has a favorable outcome, and other times, it doesn't. We all need to express a refined and consistent method of organizing our daily activities to yield positive outcomes. Developing and sharing complementary practices that repel stress and promote efficiency and effectiveness is a reasonable way to preserve homeostasis.

One extension of our daily activities that requires excellent organizational skills is in the workplace. Employment is a source of motivation and a solid vehicle that provides structure to help us achieve our very best. Our workplace represents a professional stage that allows an individual to fluidly express learned or innate skills to the fullest. It is also an environment where individuals experience additional processes or alternative methods to achieve personal growth. In many professions, daily interactions and collaboration with others is commonplace, and the need to develop solutions to existing challenges is essential. However, in order to perform at a high level each day, it is critical to build a framework of planning and organizing. Doing so will allow individuals to function, process information effectively, and execute strategies that lead to favorable outcomes.

Some may become overwhelmed and say, "With so many stimuli around me each day, it's hard for me to stay focused and organized. How can I process what I have learned most effectively? Do I have a plan to put me on course to achieve all my objectives? What resources are available to assist me?" These are a few questions that surface when thinking about becoming organized in our daily activities including the workplace.

Staying centered and focused on any objective requires a learned ability to filter out external distractions. Our minds are constantly at work, processing lots of signals, so it's easy to become diverted to what is going on around us ... our environment. We have to accept the fact that we cannot learn everything at once.

YOU DON'T HAVE TO KNOW EVERYTHING

Have you ever participated in a class, seminar, or program that goes on for hours? Regardless of how talented the presenter of the material is, there comes a point of diminishing returns, where you can no longer absorb, and you need a mental break to process the information. For people of all ages, learning is a process. As I mentioned earlier, it requires repetition, but it also requires space and time to absorb. A former colleague in the pharmaceutical industry had a great phrase to help emphasize that point. We would sit next to each other at meetings, and the segments would go on for a couple of hours before taking a break. He leaned over to me at one meeting and whispered, "I guess they don't realize that the mind can only absorb what the ass can bear." How true! We can become distracted, our minds will wander, and we can only tolerate a download of information in limited increments. We need time to digest information provided and clear space in our minds to stay in balance. Yet with the right approach, careful planning, organization, and time, we can process information readily and achieve our daily objectives.

Plenty of resources are available today to assist us in our planning and organizing efforts. As example, we now have the luxury of using the internet to explore tools to help us plan our day and review information on the value of being organized. Additionally, in the workplace there are training and development functions to facilitate employee growth by becoming adroit in organizational and planning behaviors. Being serious about being organized is the first step in building behavioral strength in this important competency. By incorporating what we learn on our own, in training, and through trial and error, we can position ourselves favorably in meetings and exceed our work responsibilities.

In thinking about planning, organizing, and processing information effectively, I also recall an important message I received in 1978 as a freshman at Fordham University from my biology professor, Father Sullivan. He told us that we were going to receive plenty of information during his class, and we should not try to remember everything. What he said has stuck with me and helped me progress in capably earning my degree and advancing in the workplace. He said, "You don't have to know everything; you just have to know where to find the information." That simple sentence helped put me and many others at ease. We realized we could not retain large amounts of information provided at once. However, we could listen attentively, understand the key points presented, take notes on highlights, and plan to refer to the textbook or other available resources to support our retention over time. He provided a clear recommendation on planning to be resourceful and becoming organized in the learning process.

As the patriarch and in paying homage to my fruitful upbringing, I will continue to make every effort to share my learning experiences with my family and others. They have realized the importance of planning and being organized in school or in the workplace. Unfortunately, they still have not perfected the meaning of being organized at home, as reflected in the disarray within their bedrooms. I guess my admonishments and ongoing requests are filled with too much information, and they cannot absorb what I intended to convey. I am confident that they will learn to use their resources effectively to assist them in becoming more appropriately organized within their living space.

My asking "When do you plan to put all your crap away?" has not yielded a favorable outcome to date, so I need to try an alternative approach. I may consider rescinding their iPhone for some time, but that may trigger a series of unnecessary distractions that will only compound the dilemma. I could resort to the tactics my parents incorporated, but then I will have to pay exorbitant hospitalization costs.[25] So what do you do? You *go to work* … and let them live in their quagmire.

---

[25] Nah … just kidding.

GO TO WORK

If we think of education in terms of preparing us for adulthood, then it's safe to assume that eventually, all young students will go off to work. But why are we habituated to have to *go to work*? Is it because that is what we learned from those around us? Is it simply for survival, as we need to earn in order to eat and provide for others and ourselves? That's obvious yet not the full story. Perhaps it is something more meaningful—a drive that prompts us to want to seek employment.

First, we are most likely programmed to work, and like the billions of people who have come before us, we have become accustomed to the history and culture of work traditions. From a historical perspective, take a look at the Bible; you can trace the origins of work back to the teachings in Genesis.

> Thus the heavens and the earth were finished, and all their multitude. And on the seventh day God finished the work he had done, and he rested on the seventh day from the work he had done ... And the Lord God formed man of the dust of the ground, and breathed into his nostrils the breath of life; and man became a living soul ... And the Lord God planted a garden eastward in Eden; and there he put man whom he had formed. And the Lord God took the man, and put him into the garden of Eden to till it and to keep it.[26]

Next, from a cultural aspect, we all seek work. Work is important and gives us a sense of purpose ... something to which we aspire. Work is part of God's original plan and design for the human spirit. When we work hard, sacrifice, and accomplish a work objective, we become fulfilled and content. Work makes us feel more secure. We develop confidence and build character and integrity. Work plays a significant role in our development, and it behooves all of us to find solace and

---

[26] Genesis 2; 1:2; 7:8; 15 (KJV).

strength in the workplace. Everyone should be able to draw from work the means of providing for family and self and serving the community.

If work is so important to us, why, then, do most people feel encumbered by having to follow a daily routine of going to work? Many people view work as a monotonous, valueless chore. If it were not for earning pay, individuals would not want to engage in the practice. In fact, most people feel that way. Professor Barry Schwartz, in his book *Why We Work*, provides valuable insight into the work quandary and reveals how to take practical steps toward finding meaningful work. He says,

> A published 2013 Gallup report that measured international employee satisfaction from 230,000 full- time and part-time workers in 142 countries. Overall, Gallup found that only 13 percent of workers feel engaged by their jobs. These people feel a sense of passion for their work, and they spend their days helping move their organization forward. The vast majority of us, some 63 percent, are not engaged. We are checked *out*, sleepwalking through our days, putting little energy into our work.[27]

Gallup asked questions that captured many of the reasons why a small percentage of workers feel *engaged* by their jobs. They feel engaged because of "the opportunity to do our work 'right,' to do our best, to be encouraged to develop and learn, to feel appreciated by coworkers and supervisors, to feel that our opinions count, to feel that what we do is important, and to have good friends at work. And for the overwhelming majority of people, work falls short—very short."[28]

Through a series of exploration into individuals and their work responsibilities, Professor Schwartz accents a vision of the future of work and how we can find fulfillment by finding work that suits our

---

[27] Barry Schwartz, *Why We Work* (Simon & Schuster, 2015), 3.
[28] Ibid.

human nature. "If we design workplaces that permit people to do the work they value, we will be designing a human nature that values work."[29]

As with educational programs in our youth, as adults, we need to seek employment opportunities that allow us to express ourselves completely and utilize our capabilities and experience to the fullest. I feel very appreciative that with almost every employment opportunity I had before, during, and after college, I was engaged. I was reassured and encouraged to develop and learn. I felt valued that my contributions were important, and I felt appreciated by my coworkers and supervisors. And with each position, I developed long-lasting, meaningful friendships.

WE ALL NEED A SHEPHERD REDUX

In the later school years, children begin to think seriously about and prepare for adult employment. During my high school years, I was fortunate to work with my brothers and friends during the summer in the New York City Youth Employment Program. Each borough across the city received an allotment of jobs for low-income youth. Our Bronx community was fortunate to participate, thanks to the efforts of Dom and Jack and their social service involvement and leadership.

Some of the responsibilities included upkeep within the community, cleaning parks and schools, monitoring and coordinating recreational activities, attending neighborhood safety-patrol meetings, and supervising other teens on field trips. These opportunities provided me with a perspective on working with others in completing assigned tasks and gaining insight into individual and group dynamics. Learning to work, both independently and within teams, was an important lesson that helped me immensely as I progressed in my employment endeavors. The by-product of earning income was also rewarding.

I worked throughout college and had a few menial jobs to earn some cash for expenses. I worked as a sales clerk at a large supply store for

---

[29] Ibid., 85–86.

toys and outdoor goods, located in the Bronx near Coop City. I ended up getting fired after a year of service because I was tossing a football in the storage area during a break. I ended up accidently knocking off a sprinkler head that caused a flood and led to a few thousand dollars' worth of destroyed merchandise. The situation was uncomfortable, for sure, yet truth be told, the management was unusual. Even though I was irritated by the incident, the outcome was not overly troublesome. As example, a director once used my shirt to wipe down his motorcycle that he liked to show off. As I was leaving the store for the last time, and the firemen were still trying to find the shutoff valve, I told him he could use my shirt again to mop up the floor.

Through these early experiences, I learned to avoid distractions and negative behaviors when in the workplace. Even though senior leaders may possess weak skills and capabilities, employees must maintain and display professionalism at all times.

My next work experience was with a distributor of the *Daily News*, a New York City newspaper. I would receive bundles of newspapers at four in the morning in the back stairwell of my building, load them in my car, and deliver them to the homes of teens with paper routes in the Bronx. This was not a good employment decision because I ended up sleeping in a few morning science classes. I realized that in order to learn, it was fairly important to stay awake and alert. Thankfully, this was a limited work encounter.

When I was a junior in college, Dom assisted me once again and introduced me to a colleague who was a youth counselor at Riverdale Neighborhood House in the Bronx. This historic social service center provides a broad spectrum of educational and community resources for preschoolers to the elderly from all socioeconomic backgrounds. I was pleased to secure employment as a youth coordinator. My supervisor, Mark, took me under his wing and helped me acclimate rapidly in working within the social service arena that was geared toward the development of youth in the community. I embraced my role and responsibilities by engaging in the social and psychological sphere of teenagers who participated in the services provided at "the Nabe." All the youth we worked with were in high schools near or within the Riverdale section of the Bronx. They were diverse in every way and challenged us in every way. I was not too far removed from their daily experiences. I was able to empathize with them, as I made a concerted effort to listen, observe, and learn as much as possible about each individual.

I had no formal education or experience in the field of social work. Yet what I did possess was a wealth of knowledge and experiences from living with young adults in a diverse neighborhood on the other side of the Bronx. Additionally, Mark was working toward a degree in psychology and counseling troubled youth. He, along with other seasoned social workers, supervised us and expedited our learning curve. They were professionals who were truly committed to providing a safe learning environment for both the teenagers served and the employees who supported their needs.

Following my graduation at Fordham University, I continued to work at Neighborhood House. At that juncture, I became fairly tentative regarding my aspirations to enter the health care field. After three years of work in the social service capacity, I was able to connect well with the staff and teenagers. A solid youth group existed. They wanted to belong to a program designated to helping them develop into capable, goal-oriented adults. I learned plenty from my interactions with each of them and was pleased they trusted and respected my efforts to support them in every way.

My supervisor recognized my progress, commitment, and genuine intentions in working with the team to provide superior service. She suggested I shift gears away from the health care field and enter the world of social service. Following her advice, I applied to Fordham University's School of Social Service and was accepted. Yet even though I was accepted, I still maintained a residual drive to find a pathway to work in the medical field in a capacity that supported patient needs.

Soon, I uncovered a niche within the health care arena that would link with my career objectives and skill sets. Cotter, a friend and softball teammate, had worked in the pharmaceutical industry for years. He thought I would be a good fit as a sales representative. As I learned more about the role and requirements, I grew more interested.

I envisioned an opportunity to bring my personal band of education in the sciences, life and work experiences, and abilities well suited for pharmaceutical sales.

And to his credit and guidance, I landed a position with Pennwalt Corporation in 1984 as an account sales representative in the Bronx. Pharmaceutical sales became an avenue for me to express what I had learned in every way up to that point. How's this for coincidence? The manager who interviewed me and subsequently hired me was Bob C., who also lived in the Bronx, had an educational background in the sciences, and lived just a few miles away on the same avenue where I grew up—Holland Avenue. In every way, Bob became a great mentor and friend. He gave me a chance to learn and grow. Under his supervision, I became very confident and acquired the requisite skills to compete and achieve.

After three fulfilling years of working in the Bronx, I became restless because I learned that Pennwalt was a target to be acquired. Bob, as a longtime employee, understood my apprehension. He told me that I was capable of transitioning to any pharma company, and he wished me nothing but the best. One of my final responsibilities was to attend a conference for family practitioners, held at the Sagamore Resort in Lake George, New York. Attending that meeting would alter my career significantly.

While at the Sagamore, I met fine coworkers and many engaging physicians, but perhaps the most important aspect of the conference was that it expanded my network of professionals from other companies. One person I was introduced to was a manager for Boehringer Ingelheim. He had keen insight into the industry and into other companies and their innovative products. Additionally, he was well versed in the news reports that indicated my company was about to be bought out, and he asked if I would be interested in meeting with one of his colleagues. I agreed and subsequently met with another manager, who was looking for a sales representative to cover the northern New Jersey territory.

My meeting with Curt was productive, and he recognized my capabilities. I was interested in the position, but I was not able to relocate to New Jersey. I explained that my father was in declining health, and I needed to remain in the New York metropolitan area. He understood and was rather empathetic. We parted ways, and some time went by before I heard from him again on October 26, 1987. This was a devastating day for my family and me, as my father had passed away. That was a somber day, yet I realized I was fortunate to have my dad with me for twenty-seven years, and I knew he was proud of the progress I'd made in building a career. When Curt called, I explained to him what had occurred. He offered his condolences and requested to meet me shortly thereafter to discuss an employment opportunity. It turns out Curt had transitioned to another company, Forest Laboratories, Inc. Forest had a subsidiary, Forest Pharmaceuticals, and he was hired as a regional director to lead a sales team in the northeast. When we met, he was already familiar with my background and was more interested in discussing a sales territory on the island of Manhattan. Up until that point, I had never worked outside of the Bronx, but I was willing to consider it.

In 1987, Forest had 159 sales representatives nationally, with just a few million dollars in sales. This was hardly a recognizable company, relative to some of the larger companies in the industry, like Pfizer, Merck, or Glaxo. Before making a final decision, I spoke with my manager, Bob C. He was pleased that I was recognized and offered a position, yet he was protective because he was not familiar with Forest. He was concerned I was making a hasty decision. I told him I was planning on making the move, and Bob supported me and offered his assistance. This was not an easy decision, but on December 14, 1987, I joined Forest Pharmaceuticals as a professional sales representative, covering all of Manhattan. This was the beginning of a long and rewarding career.

Following the training program, I was ready to get after it and start selling in the City. The job was essentially the same as the one I had in the Bronx, except in a different location, different doctors, different product categories, and under different leadership. I acclimated rather quickly and became very impressed with the senior and executive leadership of the company.

I attended my first national sales meeting and listened carefully to the presentations that outlined the company goals and strategies for growth. I was captivated with the senior executives and their innovative style of leadership, which was grounded, personable, engaging, and inclusive. I felt welcomed in the genuine familial atmosphere they created, which was refreshing and comforting. I met the VP of sales, executive VP of sales and marketing, executive VP of finance and operations, and the CEO. My introduction at that meeting would trigger numerous introductions with personnel across multiple levels. I enjoyed the role, my colleagues, and the outlook for future success and advancement.

Not long after joining Forest, I learned that Pennwalt had been acquired. Unfortunately, my good friend and former manager, Bob C., was out of a job. He asked me if there were any sales positions available; I told him I would inquire. It turned out there was a vacant position in the Bronx, and I enthusiastically recommended Bob to my manager. Bob secured the position, and after his first year with Forest, he earned the President's Club award for outstanding achievement. I was elated for Bob, yet wished I had the Bronx, as I was languishing in a soup bowl of a territory in Manhattan.

After a several years of working for Forest as a sales representative, I grew determined to advance to a supervisory role. I felt confident that I was capable of leading a team successfully, and I was eager to impart the years of sales experience gained in a capacity that suited my seasoned skill set. In the three-plus years that I was at Forest, I formed meaningful relationships with many within the sales force and within the corporate office, located in New York City. My peers and senior leaders knew the territory I worked in was a tough row to hoe. They respected my resilience and drive to achieve.

Mike, the leader of the sales team, was always one to listen and offer suggestions and words of encouragement. He became a cherished confidant, supporter, and friend. Similarly, my immediate supervisors were aware of my career objectives, and they recognized my ability to take the next step. At a sales meeting in Florida in 1990, I had a spirited and enjoyable conversation with the executive vice president of sales and marketing, Phil, who was connected with the sales force. He was integrated with the team in every way, and I soon found that he was a source of motivation, encouragement, and inspiration. He wanted the sales team to compete and excel, and he was an emblem for the sales organization.

Phil came to know of my interests firsthand and sought additional feedback from my managers. He was a well-respected mover and shaker. Phil wanted to see Forest and its players succeed. He was intense, willing to listen, eager to understand the realities on the front line, and open to suggestions for alternative approaches to the business. More important, he respected my candor and willingness to progress. He became a trustworthy shepherd.

In December 1990, I had an opportunity to work in my sales territory with a newly appointed regional director. He spent the day observing my skills, and I took the time to elicit his feedback on management. He valued my capabilities and readiness for advancement, and he was willing to consider me for the New York City division manager position. I interviewed with others for the position and earned the spot. I could not have been happier, and the new position was just one of many more leadership positions I was determined to attain.

For the next quarter of a century, I utilized skills learned in childhood to persist with patience through experiential learning. Little by little, I advanced toward my goals within the Forest organization with a variety of leadership roles.

My transition to specialty division manager propelled me to the President's Club in 1995.[30] Soon after, I was promoted to regional director for the New York metro region and capably led a larger team of sales reps and managers. I was not in this position very long before I joined two other successful leaders and good friends in the corporate office and became national director of sales in 1997. Working collaboratively with the sales and marketing teams, I helped prepare

---

[30] Interestingly enough, while leading the specialty sales team, I was pleased to supervise Bob C. I enjoyed every moment of working with him and sharing the many skills he had taught me years earlier.

and grow the company rapidly, with successful launches of blockbuster brands that changed the scope of Forest Labs. Forest was no longer a little company with a few hundred reps. We were on the edge of explosive growth and expansion to include thousands in the sales force, which positioned Forest favorably for years to come.

In 2000, I was promoted to vice president of sales, leading the sales team to record sales for our promoted brands, which eclipsed $1 billion. I helped lead the Forest team for over a decade. I collaborated well with my peers, enjoyed my job, celebrated much success, and built great friendships.

In 2005, I was promoted to senior vice president of sales, joining a strong group of executives as corporate officers for Forest Pharmaceuticals, and I was extremely proud of my accomplishments.

We competed against some of the largest companies in the pharma space. Forest was recognized as a Fortune 500 company and was considered in the industry as a major player with a fiery sales force that was held in high regard.

In every role I earned until my departure in 2014, I embraced the opportunity to learn and support the growth of the company. And beyond the joy of helping to build and lead the sales team, the one area that struck a chord for me was the training and development function. Assisting sales representatives and management on building greater capabilities can have a marked effect on yielding improved outcomes.

WORKING WITH EMOTIONAL INTELLIGENCE

One element of our sales development program I was most pleased to blend into our platform pertained to working with emotional intelligence. This critical aspect and approach to leading people to achieve greater outcomes was meaningful to me. The reason I gravitated to the logic centered on the specific method and process of teaching people the relationship of behaviors and performance. I realized the scientific foundation of emotional intelligence was anchored in my life experiences. Examples include (but are not limited to) living in a diverse, low-income community; growing up in a Bronx housing complex; learning within a disciplined, religious, educational framework; engaging in robust employment experiences; and forming many meaningful relationships.

In my view, Daniel Goleman's work on *Emotional Intelligence* and his subsequent books, *Working with Emotional Intelligence* and *Social Intelligence*, are must-reads for any individual who seeks the responsibility for leading and developing others. I will simply frame all the above as a platform for "living with emotional intelligence." Anyone can live an emotionally intelligent life. It's just a matter of committing yourself to the process of learning and improving. As it relates to working with emotional intelligence (EI), outlined below are the cornerstones that every company needs to embed in its training and development program and its competency-based performance appraisals, if it has such systems available for its employees.

Goleman expresses clearly that to succeed in life and the workplace, you need to be armed with specific competencies that will enable you to flourish and become more effective and productive. In *Working with Emotional Intelligence*, he says,

> I had the lowest cumulative grade point average in my engineering school ... But when I join the army and went to officer candidate school, I was number one in my class—it was all about how you handle yourself, get along with people, work in teams, leadership. And that's what I find is true in the world of work.[31]

After years of scientific research with many American employers on how people behave and apply their skills in the workplace, Goleman found,

> More than half the people who work for them lack the motivation to keep learning and improving in their

---

[31] Daniel Goleman, *Working with Emotional Intelligence* (Bantam Books, 1998), 4.

job. Four in ten are not able to work cooperatively with fellow employees, and just 19 percent of those applying for entry-level jobs have enough self-discipline in their work habits.[32]

In a national survey of what employers are looking for in entry-level workers, specific technical skills are now less important than the underlying ability to learn on the job. After that employers listed:

- listening and communication
- adaptability and creative responses to setbacks and obstacles
- personal management, confidence, motivation to work toward goals, a sense of wanting to develop one's career and take pride in accomplishments
- group and interpersonal effectiveness, cooperativeness and teamwork, skills at negotiating disagreements
- effectiveness in the organization, wanting to make a contribution, leadership potential[33]

Each of these employers listed competencies for me that were honed during my childhood development. The support, guidance, and education that I received from my parents, friends, and mentors within my Bronx environment helped shape and develop these central competencies and behaviors. And it is for that reason I attribute much of my professional success to the setting I embraced from birth to adulthood.

You can review the specifics contained within each of Goleman's works to better understand the emotional competence framework. For the sake of simplicity, the framework is broken out into personal and social competence. The former "consists of self-awareness,

---

[32] Ibid., 12.
[33] Ibid., 12–13.

self-regulation and motivation," whereas the latter "involves empathy and social skills or adeptness at inducing desirable responses in others."[34]

I continue to learn and apply the principles of EI each day in my daily encounters, and in doing so, I become more confident in my abilities to achieve and develop meaningful relationships.

I am forever grateful for the relationships I have built throughout my professional career, and in particular, I am indebted to the capable executives at Forest Laboratories who helped me—and thousands of others—to achieve success. Mike, Phil, Ken, and the backbone of Forest Laboratories, Howard, were the primary pioneers and champions who set the table so that all who joined could thrive. It is no coincidence that the three top executives were residents of New York City during their childhoods, and they too were exposed to the realities of their environment, which prepared them to achieve their best and succeed. Howard was a Bronx native, Phil grew up in Brooklyn, and Ken was raised in Queens. Their steadfast leadership and guidance served as motivation to do our very best to achieve … and that we did.

In all my working years, I have learned a great many lessons about basic motivations for working but also about the drive to have distinctive success. On the basic side, we have to earn to eat and provide. Further, we have to keep busy for the health of our minds and bodies. We need to have a sense of purpose and belonging. We need to satisfy our need for competition and achievements. At a higher level, when we move beyond basics, we develop a desire to be recognized for our accomplishments. We desire financial independence, security, and even wealth, if possible. Finally, on the community side, we want to be valued for our contributions to our employer and society as a whole. Working is crucial, and it fulfills needs. Although it was sometimes difficult, I'm proud of my persistence throughout the years and for the font of knowledge and success I obtained as a result.[35]

---

[34] Ibid., 26–27.

[35] I have included in the appendix an essay that many will find useful in understanding health care costs relative to prescription drugs.

CHAPTER 8

Experiential Learning: Embracing Newness

Think of early childhood education, and you will come to understand the essence of experiential learning. Experiential learning is simply the process of learning through experience.[36] Children are innocent in thought and spirit. They have no preformed views, attitudes, or impressions. They are open, truthful, and willing to learn new things, and any degree of learning comes by way of what they do, see, and hear each day. Parents are constantly answering questions their children fire at them in rapid succession.

As a parent, a simple hand-in-hand walk with my children would bring forth simple questions of what they viewed as new and interesting but what we deem as ordinary and routine. We can all learn from children by not taking for granted anything we encounter, and we can become comfortable asking lots of questions when surrounded by "newness." We can all learn by doing new things or new ways of doing old things.

The exchange of thoughts, feelings, and emotions between individuals or groups fosters learning and creates valuable memories to draw upon. At birth, children have an unadulterated brain. Their pure brains are not adult like; they're ready to imprint and capture billions and billions of new stimuli. Their brains are ripe to absorb new

---

[36] You can gain additional insight into the concept from Wikipedia. There, you will find references to the experiential learning model, implementation, application in school and business, and the overall benefits.

information and data. If you compare the human brain to a computer, a computer can archive gigabytes of information that can be retrieved when needed, but it cannot transmit data with emotions attached.

In Latin, *tabula rasa* means "blank slate." *Merriam-Webster's* definition includes "the mind in its hypothetical primary blank or empty state before receiving outside impressions; something existing in its original pristine state."

The brains of our children, at birth, exist in their original, pristine state, only to be layered with information delivered by those they encounter and what they experience independently. They learn by doing. They learn from the framework provided by their parents. Children willingly and unconsciously acclimate to the newness around them. Similarly, it is in our best interest to process what we encounter with an open and unfiltered mind.

How many times have we heard from our parents and mentors "you have to try something to learn something"? As example, when we were just a few years old, our parents would ask, "Do you want to go to the playground and go on the swings?" We may have answered affirmatively, having been to the playground, but we had no reference or recall to "the swings."[37] So it was off to the playground. We approached the swings and became anxious, having never experienced being on one. We were placed on the seat and told to hold the chains or rope attached. We were pushed and became airborne. We now knew what it meant to be on a swing because we experienced it firsthand. We could now picture it in our minds and remember the feeling of going back and forth, and with each push, we went higher and higher, creating more exhilaration. For most of us, it was a pleasant experience, yet for some, it may have been traumatic, and the thought of the swing created intense anxiety. We learned whether or not we would want to go on a swing again in the future.

---

[37] I use this example because when my father asked me if I wanted to go the playground and go on the swings, I recall the feeling of anxiety. I also recognized the same anxiety in my children when I took them to the playground for the first time.

That's what daily encounters trigger in our minds. Our experiences create a spectrum of learning that begins with a reflection, visualization, and formulation as to feelings of satisfaction or displeasure, and it concludes with a reference to engage in such an experience again. But regardless of whether we enjoyed the experience, there was concrete learning. The more we experience, the more we learn, favorable or unfavorable.

I experienced plenty of newness growing up in the Bronx and the Gun Hill projects with my family. I learned to embrace the newness and differences that existed—the differences in race, cultures, behaviors, attitudes, leadership styles, education, employment, and family values. In similar fashion, I welcomed the synergies of the family unit and religious educational structure. Most of the experiences and learning were pleasant, but those that were not stand out front and center. The pleasant experiences included the ability to form many friendships easily. There was no shortage of individuals to connect with. These friendships carried over into adulthood. At the same time, there were negative experiences of friendships formed. There were childhood friends who fell victim to alcohol abuse and drug addiction; friends who lost interest in school and opted for unfulfilling jobs; friends who seemingly lost interest in embracing what each day had to offer and suffered the hardship of depression and anxiety; or friends who were engaged in destructive behaviors, including drug usage, violence toward others, and isolation.

Usually, there was a comforting feeling of togetherness within my home and surroundings. Morning, noon, and night, there was always someone available to experience new things with, to answer my questions, and to gain insight from the daily learning. There was more than enough engagement throughout the day to keep my mind active. Meeting a new friend, attending a new event, engaging in new discussions of the incidents of the day, feisty challenges over differing opinions, and disputes within the home over who was going to clean up were routine experiences.

I enjoyed experiencing new events with my parents, brothers, sister, friends, and classmates. I also was eager to learn new things independently. Small happenings included going to the playground to see if anyone was out so we could engage in some sports or mischievous activity, running to the corner store the get the newspaper, going to the supermarket, and delivering the food or an item to a neighbor. Most of all, I enjoyed meeting new people and uncovering their likes and dislikes. As my circle of friends widened, I learned to appreciate those who shared similar viewpoints and to compromise with those who did not.

Not everything was rosy inside or outside of my home. Life happened, and I learned by interpreting what I heard, saw, and experienced within my environment. At any one time, there would be parental disagreements, sibling or interfamilial discord, challenges, fights between friends, financial hardships and its effects, and extended family privations. For example, it was not uncommon for my parents to argue over financial difficulties in meeting family needs, including a shortage of funds for tuition due or payments that needed to be made for food purchased on credit. Yet with each experience, I learned to evaluate how I would respond or approach each situation in the future.

What stood out as vivid negative experiences in the projects was witnessing the aftermath of suicide in two separate instances. In one case, a distraught, vulnerable individual jumped from a top floor of an adjacent building, instantly ending his life. Many bystanders in the vicinity either saw the act firsthand or heard the impact. When some of us approached afterward and saw the remains of a broken individual, it trigged an immediate question of why. What can go so wrong in someone's life to cause an individual to pursue personal destruction? What mental anguish can be so consuming that death or physical degradation is the preferred alternative?

Similar questions arise when recalling another instance where an individual took his life in the same fashion. A hallucinatory drug effect was the cause. At the time, drug consumption in the neighborhood was rampant; heroine and its debilitating effects manifested in a variety of ways, most of which resulted in physical and mental harm. Such glaring experiences remain fixed in my mind and keep me cognizant of the fragile nature of the human spirit and the impact of experiences we encounter.

Experiencing newness is a double-edged sword, yet with each unveiled episode comes a learning that remains etched in our minds for as long as we chose to draw upon its value. We repress some frequencies of newness and keep them locked away for decades or forever. Any recollection of a negative or traumatic event brings forward too much pain and despair, whereas thought-provoking, refreshing, and rewarding experiences trigger an alternative response that moves us to a higher level of satisfaction.

An extension of newness, in today's parlance, is associated with something that is fresh or that can activate a rush of gratification—perhaps a new car, iPhone, computer, high-tech TV, video game, pair of shoes, or any other item that is in vogue. Got to have it ... got to try it. Such new items are novelties and generate a pseudouplift. Over time, however, the item or experience once desired becomes ordinary, and the drive to seek a new gadget kicks in, and the cycle repeats itself.

A NEW PROGRAM

A reprogramming toward seeking gratification from a new experience that serves as a catalyst for change *to assist others* is required. We can establish the creation of a mind-set where we focus our thoughts and emotions away from our self-driven motives and channel our energies toward the growth and development of others. Our children are extremely desirous of experiencing newness, and they long for parental guidance, direction, and counsel as they explore their world of newness.

Embracing newness as an unfamiliar experience that brings about personal value or meaning can be expressed favorably to assist in the development of others. This is a perspective worth understanding. As example, forming an alternative approach to motivate and inspire our youth to achieve is representative of the type of newness we need to cultivate. Or serving as a liaison to bridge division within a community can be personally rewarding. We can think of novel ways to explore newness and engage in experiences that yield favorable outcomes for others.

For centuries, the human spirit has been propelled to seek newness. The quest for fire was an experience for cavemen that changed the course of events in a significant way. Our first explorers—Christopher Columbus, Ferdinand Magellan, Henry Hudson, and others—chartered new waters to seek new lands, cultures, and provisions. They encountered the vast newness that we all grasp today. Space exploration was a goal we were unwilling to forgo, and it served to whet our appetite for understanding our universe. Our drive to enhance the human condition in every way has continued throughout the ages, and it serves to bring greater strength and peace to everyone.

We are all curious; we want to explore and learn new things. This desire to advance and experience newness is automatic. This quest for newness is a programmed learning mechanism. Our human nature demands that we explore new things, to be eternally curious. We have all participated in experiential learning since birth. We received input from our environment, we evaluated or interpreted the experience, and there was an outcome, favorable or unfavorable. Either way, we learned from the experience we were presented with. Think about the learning you experienced from your childhood—the environment you were exposed to, the family support and education you received, and your work experiences. What stands out as most favorable? What was not so pleasant? What would you like to have changed, or what support would you have appreciated? Most of us can recall our childhood experiences clearly. And if we give careful thought to the events or circumstances experienced, we can make an effort to refine or alter our approach when confronted with similar life experiences. Each of us participated in different forms of learning through experience.

From a traditional educational sense, experiential learning can be divided into two categories: field-level experiences and classroom learning. As example, field-level learning is perhaps the most conventional form and can include participation in community-based programs, seminars, internships, and supplemental education programs. Classroom-type experiential learning varies and can include presentations, role-playing, case studies, simulations, and group work exercises. This type of learning is very common in the workplace and can play a supportive role in bolstering competence.

Who benefits from experiential learning? There are at least two beneficiaries: the learner and the educating body (institutions, universities, organizations). To have a successful outcome, experiential learners need to possess a willingness to interpret their experience on an issue or topic independently.[38] They can reflect reason for themselves and be able to articulate their position effectively. They need to formulate a motivation for the experience they are undertaking and to maintain the discipline and self-management skills to work alone or in groups. Experiential learners need to be open-minded and able to work with people who offer different views. Organizations or universities become stronger and more productive from their learners' experiences. The learner becomes more equipped with the knowledge and skill necessary to compete and advance.

In life, school, and the workplace, we are bombarded with newness and opportunities for experiential learning. In order to reap the favorable benefits of each experience, we can be prepared to accept and be open to the experiences we encounter. We can reflect on each experience, outline how we can progress or learn from newness, and become mentally resilient in withstanding any new experience. Ultimately, we can interpret the value from each experience and encourage those we interact with each day. Embracing the newness you face will add a supplemental layer of knowledge for you to draw upon, as needed. Gaining understanding of newness will enhance your development and those you lead.

Much of my success has come from my drive to overcome fear of new experiences, and this trait is sorely needed today. It's not always easy to get ahead, but it's always worth it to try, whether for the experience only or for the experience and success. Persistence and courage are key.

---

[38] For children, this might be after-school programs for supplemental learning. For adults, it might be participation in seminars on relevant topics.

CHAPTER 9

Death's Value

Losing loved ones, those who shaped your childhood development and put you on the right path to achieve great things, is hard to endure. Losing parents in adulthood has an extreme impact on how you choose to progress in every facet of life. At the same time, making the most of the worst experience in life can be fulfilling and can assist you in becoming spiritually resilient and more determined to find inner peace through a loving desire to blossom.

From the outside, this framing on the death of loved ones sounds interesting, but in reality, we may wonder how we can adjust to make life more meaningful and gratifying following such a foreign and negative experience. The answer for each of us is unique, because we all maintain an individualized recollection of the special and valuable wisdom gained from each parent we loved. Lessons, beliefs, and experiences are takeaways that we can advance in the absence of our parents. The spirit and memory of how they lived their lives and guided us to achieve is ever-present. We draw upon that reservoir to keep us whole, mindful, and prepared to live our lives to the fullest. Without that base, life's challenges can seem daunting and insurmountable.

Death is the end of life on earth; it's final. All that we are—the thoughts and feelings we have—is erased when we die. It's no wonder that most people find discussions on the topic uncomfortable and pointless. What brings meaning to life, in all its glory, is the fact that we are aware that we will die at some point. How we choose to live life, through lessons learned from those before us, is what defines and brings unique joy to living. Our faith gives purpose and meaning to our lives. Our faith gives structure to living our lives in peace with those around us. And as referenced earlier, in the absence of peace and order, we have chaos, destruction, and evil. Living life through peace, harmony, and love is the favored choice.

We learn to experience life from the time we take our first breath. We are cared for and protected by our parents, and as we develop, we become oriented to the virtues and beliefs that shape our character. We learn a belief system accepted by our parents and displayed for us each day until they die. We acquire values that we keep alive in their absence so the cycle of love, devotion, and faith remains alive for generations.

Our faith, parents, and family are what keeps us active and capable of shaking off any murk. I know that was a vital support system that helped me embrace my surroundings and grow in confidence. I enjoyed a dynamic childhood and formed great memories of my parents—memories I can cherish for a lifetime.

A SOMBER AUTUMN MORNING

I was born in 1960, when my father was fifty-three and my mother was thirty-three years of age. Growing up, I knew that my mother would be with me for a good while, but I was anxious and uncertain about how near death was for my father. My parents didn't really live hard; they went to the doctor as needed, yet perhaps not as often as they should have; and they lived modestly. Even if they had wanted to live aggressively, they couldn't because they did not have the means.

Upon my birth, my father had lived over 70 percent of his life, based on the life expectancy at that time. I thought of his age often and worried about when he would become ill and incapable of maintaining his strength and vigor. During my childhood years, my father was intense, stern, demanding, and highly specific in his expectations for us. He was a type-A personality, a true perfectionist. At the same time, he was loving, caring, and entirely supportive of our efforts.

I was a senior in high school when my father retired from the US Postal Service in 1977. He was seventy years of age then, yet remained in decent shape. His demeanor was noticeably subdued—not as demanding and less rigid. He laughed more often and was not as tense. He tried to enjoy each day and was not excessively concerned about the immediate needs of each family member. He spent more time alone because we were in school or at work, and he had time to reflect on his life experiences up to that point. He became very introspective, and he verbalized his past and his involvement with the family.

He was more cerebral and less reactive.

He tried to keep busy during the day, finding chores to do around the house; on weekends he would help my brother Gary with renovations at his new home in New Rochelle. The skills he honed many years earlier were still evident with his newfound attempts at masonry and carpentry, and he took great pride in his contributions.

In 1981, we had an opportunity to move from the projects. Clearly, this was not an easy decision, but with my father's retirement, finances were compressed. Also, the rents at the Gun Hill housing projects were increasing significantly as a result of Housing Authority policy changes designed to level set costs for incoming residents with existing tenants. After almost three decades of forming great friendships and living in a vibrant neighborhood in the Bronx, my family transitioned to an apartment building three miles north in Bronxville, New York. Not a great leap, but a change from what was customary nonetheless.

Getting used to our new neighborhood and confines didn't take too long. My mom blended in rapidly and had friends in the area that she continued to work with. In general, not much changed for most of us because we had cars at that point, and we could continue our daily routines. For my dad, however, a new environment and being alone for most of the day took some getting used to. A few years later, my uncle and my brother Gary and his family moved into the same building, so that kept Dad somewhat active.

Over time, we started to notice a decline in his attentiveness, and he began to feel the effects of emphysema and prolonged hypertension. He ended up getting a pacemaker and couldn't really exert himself. I accompanied him to various doctors, and his gait was wavering; he was increasingly dependent on me for support and stabilization. In addition to his progressive physical decline, his dementia weakened his mental abilities. Slowly, he was wearing down. Eventually, he suffered his first stoke, and his tentativeness in maintaining activities of daily living became increasingly apparent. Throughout his decline, however, his good nature revealed itself in all its fervor, even though he was a shell of himself. Although he made mild improvements, his second stroke was more debilitating, and it was one he could not recover from. He passed away peacefully, early in the morning of an autumn day, October 26, 1987.

For the first time since the early fifties, our family was fractured, and the loss of our father marked a central change. His death was a sobering reality for all of us. He had been a source of strength, reliability, and adoration. Losing him created an undeniable void. Our mother lost her husband and partner, and we all lost a trusted and loved guardian. There was an emotional tone that signaled the finality of our relationship to our father. And in our own ways, each of us subtly questioned how the family would change, as well as questioning our attachment to our mom and to each other.

Our family was always very tight-knit, and that was a result of the foundation established by both parents. Any one of my family and extended family members would say with confidence that even with the loss of our father, the bonds of love and strength still remained entrenched. Sure, we needed time to adjust to our loss, but we became united to help each other heal. We buoyed each other in every way. Susan was my pillar of love and support throughout, and we shared the joy of my dad's love and affection. Our loved ones and friends played an integral role in our healing process. They were very accommodating and gracious in listening and offering companionship.

In her book *Losing Your Parents, Finding Your Self*, Victoria Secunda discusses survival mechanisms and the role they play in how we progress and cope, depending on our relationships with a parent. She highlights a psychological perspective on the matter and says,

> Among Freud's loyal opponents is British psychiatrist John Bowlby, who advanced the idea that "attachment behavior"—informed by both biology and by childhood experience—explains human interactions throughout life. Bowlby believes that when parents provide their children with a "secure base" of love and encouragement, the children can confidently go out into the world because they know—and take for granted—that they have a safe place to which they can return in times of trouble. This secure base becomes the model for healthy attachments later in life, because the child has "internalized" it and made it on his or her own.[39]

In essence, we keep the love of a parent alive by living and enjoying what life has to offer. We carry forward what we learned from our parents and through our experiences. We become increasingly motivated to preserve the spirit of love through our familial safe haven, and we overcompensate for the deficit created. My other siblings were married but lived in the neighborhood. I was the only remaining child living with my mother, and when I married, my mother was alone. My uncle and brother were still living in the same apartment building and were available to assist her and support her as needed, but she was living alone for the first time in over forty years.

When my father passed on, it was recognizable that each sibling made a concerted effort to find solace in each other. This was refreshing because one of the common pleas from both of my parents was, "Always remain connected, engaged, and close to each other." Our bonds did, in fact, remain fixed, much to the delight of our family. Even through the turbulent tides that death yielded, in our case, the

---

[39] Victoria Secunda, *Losing Your Parents, Finding Your Self* (Hyperion, 2000), 15–16.

rising tides lifted all boats. We were determined to advance through life with the same strength and security we came to know throughout our childhood. Even though we were living in different places, we still preserved the nucleus of our family and remained committed to growing together as a family unit.

THE WINDS OF CHANGE

My mother carried on with her daily routines at home and work and with family and friends. She became more dependent on each of her children to support her emotionally and to help stabilize her life that was now out of balance. Katherine continued to work at Alexander's, the same department store she began working in some twenty years prior. The only difference was that in the past, she would trudge to work in the Bronx; now she would commute to her new location in Westchester County. Working each day gave my mom a mental reprieve from her ongoing thoughts of loneliness and belonging. Her life was different, but she was able to frame her circumstances around her children, in-laws, grandchildren, and friends. She eventually learned to adapt, reflect on her life, and cling to memories of old and new surroundings.

To alleviate some of the effects of our shared loss, my siblings and I made the effort to reach out to her often, join her for dinner, and try to include her in events wherever possible. Fortunately, my brothers (Gary, Gregory, and Geoff) and their families lived in close proximity to our mother and would try to keep her active when they were not at work. My sister, Nancy, and my nephews would visit at times. They would recall fond times spent with my dad and talk about what was happening in their lives.

It's hard for anyone to adjust to not having a beloved parent available to speak to, share in joyful occasions, or to seek advice from. It was difficult for me to adjust to that reality when I was planning to be married. That experience was an awakening. Susan and I had a very positive relationship with my father, and knowing that he would not be present at our wedding was disheartening. In any event, his spirit was very alive and present when we were married in the Bronx at Immaculate Conception Church on an autumn day, October 14, 1989.

Susan and I moved to Mount Kisco, New York, after we were married, and shortly thereafter, Daniel was born. Living in a new residence up north, starting a new position in management, and raising an active boy did not curtail face-to-face visits to my mom. We made every effort to join her or have her spend weekends at our new home. We were elated when we had our first child, and Mom and Susan's parents would join us in our home frequently. As our family grew, we followed the same procedure, and so did my siblings. We engaged and connected with the expanded family as often as we could, and we created new memories while drawing upon those that had shaped us.

Over the years, though my mother experienced loss as the family broke off,[40] the births of new Azzaris grew the family with an increasing number of grandchildren for our mom. She was very pleased to enjoy the company of a broader family, and in reciprocal fashion, they were pleased to grow in her presence as well. Then, after working for over a quarter of a century at Alexander's Department Store, she decided to put aside her sales talents and retire. She became tired of the commute; she felt physically diminished and had soured to the grind of the workplace. She had put in her time and had a good run, and now she wanted to spend more time with her growing family. She was proud to have worked for so long and contributing to supporting the needs of her family. We appreciated every bit of it and were thankful she was able to stay the course for so long.

Despite the stress my mom had endured since her early twenties, she maintained fairly decent health, although she wrestled with bouts of anxiety and had persistent hypertension and diabetes. Doctor visits and medication had helped maintain her health to that point, yet there were glimpses of decline setting in. In between family visits or meeting

---

[40] In October 1990, my brother Gary and his family moved and established residency in New City, New York. My sister, Nancy, and my brothers Greg and Geoff were still nearby, and they also made concerted efforts to keep Mom in close view.

with friends, her routine included breakfast, TV, babysitting, shopping, preparing dinner, more TV, and sleep. Not overly exciting, but this represented her life activities postretirement.

My brother Gary also recognized her progressive decline and thought it would be in her best interest to join him and his family at their home in Rockland County. He slowly built a capacious extension and shed to accommodate her, and in 1995, she moved from Bronxville. After some time, she acclimated to her new confines in Rockland County, and her life took on a significant twist. She was always a provider, worker, and doer for her family. Now, she was primarily on the receiving end. While she deserved and had earned her treatment, the inactivity made her feel she was stagnating and advanced her mental decline.

In 1996, there was a subtle uptick in her activities when my brother Greg, his wife, Karen, and their children also decided to move to Rockland County, just a few exits from where Gary and my mother lived. Now, Mom had another family to join in with and to relish the daily events. She kept busy between each family by babysitting, helping out where she could, and trying to stay clear of any interfamilial differences. Nancy, Geoff, and I would bring our families to visit whenever possible, and the larger family gatherings were enjoyable for us and certainly for Mom. This was her new reality and one we all grew accustomed to.

My mother was alone a lot during the day, as everyone had school and work. She was eager to see everyone when they returned home, but with both families having put in a full day, sometimes the enthusiasm was dampened.[41] In any event, everyone did their best to adapt, and together they progressed with care, and we appreciated their warm intentions and effort.

The year 1998 was one of change for my entire family. Some changes were for the better, and others were life-altering. I was

---

[41] It's not easy to have a parent attached to an extended family and in-laws. A significant give-and-take is required, sacrifices are made, and the needs of the receiving parent are, at times, minimized.

fortunate to receive a promotion and join the senior sales leadership team at Forest Labs. We were introducing a new antidepressant into the US marketplace, which required lots of strategic planning, meetings, and follow-up to ensure a successful launch. We had a great kick-off with the sales team, setting the stage for what would become one of the most successful product launches in pharmaceutical history and a significant building block for Forest.

On the home front, after nine years of curbed townhouse living, we were cautiously optimistic about shifting gears and uprooting our family to a new home a few miles way. The move, however, did not progress without some anxiety. The kids were established in school, and they would now have to change to schools where they didn't know a soul. However, if there was ever a time to make such a move, it was then, because our kids were very young and capable of adjusting rapidly. As parents, we questioned the move, as we had been entrenched for almost a decade in our previous familiar environment. Yet like most instances regarding change, we learned to adapt and embrace the newness and everything that came with it.

One change that occurred in that same year that was not fruitful but rather devastating was when Nancy had her second stroke and became nonambulatory, with seriously compromised speech. She spent some time being treated in a hospital in the Bronx and then was placed into a nursing facility. Our family would visit her, and on every trip, we would see the fear and anxiety in her eyes. We would make every attempt to comfort her and try to raise her spirits, considering her limited physical abilities and mental state. We all had a difficult time accepting our sister's altered state of being and tried to offer her encouragement and peace.

Seeing my sister deteriorate physically took a sizable chunk of life and spirit from my mother. Nancy's health circumstances enlightened all of us to the realities and frailties of the human condition, and it emboldened each of us to embrace the beauty of what life offers. We all should pursue living a life bolstered by love and vitality because we never know from one day to the next if we will have that choice.

Over time, my mother's daily routines became measured and diminished, and her health declined steadily. She became short of breath, forgetful, and disinterested in engaging. In 2001, she was hospitalized and required heart bypass surgery. She weathered the storm and even though her cardiovascular system was refreshed, her concomitant senile dementia continued to progress. Her system was out of balance. She made some strides through rehabilitation, but it eventually became apparent that she would require long-term nursing home support. Initially, she resisted the idea of being in a "home," but she gradually realized it was the best option for her, considering her shallow mental and physical states.

In 2002, my mother was permanently admitted into Cabrini Nursing Home in Dobbs Ferry, New York. Shortly after she became a resident, we made arrangements to have Nancy transferred from her Bronx nursing facility to join my mother at Cabrini. There, they lived in close proximity on the second floor, just a few feet apart, in rooms overlooking the Hudson River.

Over the next eight years, we tried to maintain our family life with our mother and sister in a familiar way under a different roof. I recall my many visits to their new home. Even though their new residence was a somber one, compared to the lively home they once had shared, we engaged them and tried to bring to life family milestones and holiday celebrations. In essence, we wanted them to experience as much of life as they could withstand, and we made every effort to keep them centered in love and affection. We wanted them to feel and sense the same love, affection, and strength they provided each of us throughout their lives. They embodied love and sacrifice, and we were indebted to them and desirous of bringing them peace.

In 2010, my mother and sister became weak, fragile, and prepared to find peace through the Holy Spirit. Mom passed peacefully on March 13, 2010, and a gestation period later, Nancy joined her mom in paradise on December 25, 2010. I will never forget that Christmas Day when en route to see my sister for the last time. The sun's rays fanned through the dark clouds vibrantly and welcomed a loving, wonderful soul. They both entered into an eternal kingdom of peace and love, and their spirits will remain alive and with us forever.

HEALING THROUGH GIVING

Through the experience of death and loss, we learn to share love with those we cherish and adore. We learn to willingly sacrifice and give to our family a new generation—a loving experience they can embrace and replicate. We can teach, guide, and support our young to live life to the fullest by caring for others and being one with each other through faith.

Victoria Secunda, in *Losing Your Parents, Finding Yourself*, suggests that the overwhelming lesson derived from the stories and experiences of those who lost loved ones is twofold: "First, the deaths of parents alter who we are now—adults who are defined by what we make of ourselves rather than those that made us. Second, this redefinition allows us to develop a new kind of love, whether in the company of others or alone."[42]

Death's value is immeasurable and can only be realized in the presence of love and understanding. Children within every community should have the chance to recognize and experience the unfiltered love of two parents, and when they do, we can rest assured that our world will be a more peaceful and productive place in which to live.

[42] Ibid, 137.

Peace

CHAPTER 10

Regeneration

Merriam-Webster.com defines *regeneration* as "an act or the process of regenerating: the state of being regenerated; spiritual renewal or revival; renewal or restoration of a body, bodily part, or biological system after injury or as a normal process."

For the purposes and context of the messages brought forward in this guide, regeneration is *a renewal of the American spirit and a rebirth of a culture that promotes parental engagement and personal responsibility.*

All of us are the biological representation and progeny of our parents. That is, we are the descendants of those who came before us in body and soul. There are some aspects of biological expression, by way of DNA, that we cannot adjust, but specific elements, including our thoughts, emotions, and behaviors are within our direct control. How we choose to express our thoughts and behaviors when guiding our children has a profound impact on how they will conduct themselves throughout the development process.

We have an opportunity to bring forward core fundamentals, beliefs, and learning from our parents when guiding the young in our lives. We also have an opportunity to break off from their parenting style and develop our own, in an expression of our independence and wisdom as parents, providing a unique foundation for supporting the development of our children. In either case, we are charged with no greater responsibility than leading our youth in a manner that allows them to display behaviors and talents confidently and prepares them to contribute to society peacefully.

Recognizing and incorporating the platform of this Bronx logic into your childhood development efforts will produce a confident generation of leaders, capable of realizing success. A renewal of prideful youth will eagerly flourish and progress into adulthood, armed with the knowledge and skills to compete and advance in life and the workplace.

Regenerating a tipping point toward parental security is paramount. *Parenting* is a reasonably sound focal point to lead children to succeed within a peaceful society. As a nation, we are overdue; it's time to reclaim the responsibility of parenting our children and put aside a self-centered approach to childhood development.

Communicate the need for *selfless parenting*. Here are some trends to ponder:

- Parenting has become an elective.
- We live in a society where anything goes … with no limits.
- Immediate gratification rules the day in communication and behaviors.
- An egocentric, self-centered, narcissistic mind-set is prevalent.
- A spiritual void is palpable.
- Social media rules as a form of communication and learning.
- Drug abuse is rampant and ordinary.
- Violence in many urban communities is on the rise.
- Educational performance is weakened in broken families.
- Social challenges from decades past are consistently renewed.
- "About 15 million children are living in poverty."[43]

There are positives trends as well, including these:

- the extension and quality of life that results from advances in medicine

---

[43] http://www.nccp.org/topics/childpoverty.html.

- technological progress
- revitalized economic growth
- low unemployment rates

Yet highlighting the distinct societal misfortunes that weigh down our country serves as a barometer to awaken the masses and prevent further erosion. That's why we have to understand the root cause of our difficulties and weaknesses. Parenting and educating our young more effectively, in all communities, can stimulate change and direct our youth toward achieving personal success.

How did we get to this point, and why are our youth repeating similar behaviors as five decades earlier? If we are, in fact, versed on the issues at hand that are related to the structure of American families, then why haven't we moved the needle? What gets in the way? Who gets in the way?

We have to define and enact practical solutions to redirect our youth toward improving their circumstances to achieve success in America. Before outlining potential solutions, we need to consider the state of the family unit in our country. With the erosion of the two-parent household, we have evolved from an American culture of belonging to one of rejection, and our children are bearing the load.

Research shows that children can develop favorably if they grow up in two-parent households. Children of intact families are less likely to experience emotional or academic deficiencies or to live in poverty.

Dr. Jane Anderson is clinical professor of pediatrics at the University of California, San Francisco. Her 2014 article, "The Impact of Family Structure on the Health of Children: Effects of Divorce," appeared in the *Linacre Quarterly*, a bioethics journal that explores issues at the interface of medicine and religion. She presents the following:

> Nearly three decades of research evaluating the impact of family structure on the health and well-being of children demonstrates that children living with their married, biological parents consistently have better physical, emotional, and academic well-being.

Pediatricians and society should promote the family structure that has the best chance of producing healthy children. The best scientific literature to date suggests that, with the exception of parents faced with unresolvable marital violence, children fare better when parents work at maintaining the marriage. Consequently, society should make every effort to support healthy marriages and to discourage married couples from divorcing.[44]

Dr. Anderson clarifies the effects of divorce on children in a logical and practical manner when she says, "Each child and each family are obviously unique, with different strengths and weaknesses, different personalities and temperaments, and varying degrees of social, emotional, and economic resources, as well as differing family situations prior to divorce. Despite these differences divorce has been shown to diminish a child's future competence in all areas of life, including family relationships, education, emotional well-being, and future earning power."[45]

In another 2014 study, "Where Is the Land of Opportunity? The Geography of Intergenerational Mobility in the United States," Raj Chetty and his colleagues from Harvard University and the University of California–Berkeley examined opportunity and economic mobility in the United States. They cited family structure as one of five key factors for economic mobility across generations. Specifically, they found significantly less mobility for individuals from single-parent households. "Family structure correlates with upward mobility not just at the individual level but also at the community level, perhaps because the stability of the social environment affects children's outcomes more broadly."[46]

---

[44] https://www.ncbi.nlm.nih.gov/pmc/articles/PMC4240051/.

[45] Ibid.

[46] http://nber.org/papers/w19843 (accessed May 16, 2016).

Additionally, the Heritage Foundation's Robert Rector has made a similarly compelling case for the antipoverty significance of intact families in his report, "Marriage: America's Greatest Weapon against Child Poverty." He estimates that marriage reduces the probability of child poverty by more than 80 percent. Rector emphasizes,

> Marriage remains America's strongest anti-poverty weapon, yet it continues to decline. As husbands disappear from the home, poverty and welfare dependence will increase, and children and parents will suffer as a result. Since marital decline drives up child poverty and welfare dependence, and since the poor aspire to healthy marriage but lack the norms, understanding, and skills to achieve it, it is reasonable for government to take active steps to strengthen marriage. Just as government discourages youth from dropping out of school, it should provide information that will help people to form and maintain healthy marriages and delay childbearing until they are married and economically stable.[47]

The data is clear, yet society continues to mask familial degradation as a cultural aberration. In an attempt to maintain political correctness and soften these apparent trends, we promote the progressive decline of America's youth. When fathers and mothers accept each other in marriage, their children are more likely to thrive. Conversely, when parents reject each other, their children may not thrive, and many falter.

It is also important to note that children within intact families can experience challenges similar to those of single parents. As example, in environments where both parents work as a means of achieving their

---

[47] https://www.heritage.org/poverty-and-inequality/report/marriage-americas-greatest-weapon-against-child-poverty.

financial and lifestyle goals, children can experience internalized and externalized behavioral stresses.

Carolyn J. Heinrich is professor of Public Affairs, an affiliated professor of Economics, and the director of the Center for Health and Social Policy at the Lyndon B. Johnson School of Public Affairs, University of Texas at Austin. Her article, "Parents' Employment and Children's Wellbeing," appeared in the 2014 spring issue of *Future of Children*. She writes,

> But parents' (and especially mothers') work, is not unambiguously beneficial for their children. On the one hand, working parents can be positive role models for their children, and, of course, the income they earn can improve their children's lives in many ways. On the other hand, work can impair the developing bond between parents and young children, especially when the parents work long hours or evening and night shifts. The stress that parents bring home from their jobs can detract from their parenting skills, undermine the atmosphere in the home, and thereby introduce stress into children's lives.[48]

Rather telling in her article was that she examined the implications of parents working and their children's well-being. Professor Heinrich offers insight into research on the topic and notes, "Biology interacts with physical and social environments to shape a child's pathways and achievements. In this sense, the time that parents—both mothers and fathers—spend caring for children is likely to influence a child's development well beyond the initial bonding period, and in different ways depending on the children's age and circumstances. Parents' work can affect all of this."[49]

---

[48] https://pdfs.semanticscholar.org/6a30/12e9f7bd125f9faff9790ee79 be9a698d871.pdf.

[49] Ibid.

She points out, "Researchers have documented that children are more likely to spend time without parental supervision at younger ages if their parents are working, which may in turn harm the children's performance in school and increase their participation in risky behaviors. Theories of how parents function and nurture their children suggest that ongoing stress at work may cause parents to withdraw from interacting with their children at home, or to be more vulnerable to stimuli that trigger conflict with their children."[50]

Professor Heinrich effectively frames the research and concludes, "The healthy development of children consistently shows that children need stable family relationships, with adults who are responsive, nurturing, and protective; physically safe environments that allow them to explore without risk or fear of harm; and adequate nutrition and health care."[51]

"Social Behaviour" is an article written in 2018 by No Isolation, a Norwegian company with a mission to reduce involuntary loneliness and social isolation. The topic reinforces the basic need of human beings for social support, care, relationships, and behavior.

> Creating social relationships is central to human well-being, and not just due to the pure joy of being with friends, or when learning social norms. It is argued that experiencing social behaviour, and engaging in social interaction, is vital during childhood development. However, many children, for various reasons, are not able to participate in, or experience, the social behaviour that is crucial for their well-being, mental health, and development.[52]

The commentary references research on the association of parental separation in childhood. "The absence of social relationships and

---

[50] Ibid.

[51] Ibid.

[52] https://www.noisolation.com/global/research/how-does-social-isolation-affect-a-childs-mental-health-and-development.

behaviours has been shown to affect child development in various ways. For example, previous research has revealed that socially isolated children tend to have lower subsequent educational attainment, be part of a less advantaged social class in adulthood, and are more likely to be psychologically distressed in adulthood (Lacey, Kumari & Bartley 2014)."[53]

Altering the effects of childhood isolation is a significant undertaking. Yet it would not be the first time that society pivoted to create meaningful change. We can start the process by speaking out vociferously on the issue at hand and to restore our environment toward a culture of belonging. We can aim for a culture that centers on reestablishing value in our country, where people and families belong to each other and parents belong to each other.

"Healing our society includes the fundamental elements that create a peaceful culture, i.e., faith and worship, traditional dating, marriage, families forming vibrant communities, and neighborhoods where loving relationships and marriage are commonplace. That's what children need today. Our children need to belong, they need to be nourished and they need to be encouraged by their parents."[54]

In comparing the numbers of children, ages fifteen to seventeen, who have either lived in always-intact or broken households, the Index of Family Belonging and Rejection, using 2008–2012 data from the US Census Bureau's American Community Survey, found that the rates of divorce and extramarital childbearing "are on the rise and two-parent families are in decline for young Americans. The index of belonging (46%) and rejection (54%) is an indicator of the social health of America."[55]

---

[53] Ibid.

[54] FamilyFacts.org.

[55] Patrick Fagan and Christina Hadford, *Fifth Annual Index of Family Belonging and Rejection* (2-12-15). http://marri.us/research/research-papers/fifth-annual-index-of-belonging-and-rejection. The statistics forming the Index of Belonging and Rejection are based on analyses of the Census Bureau's 2008–2012 American Community Survey public use file.

More specifically, 46 percent of the teenagers studied were raised in an intact family, where both biological parents were married before the child's birth. On the other side, "54% of teenagers live in families where their biological parents have rejected each other. The families with a history of rejection include single-parent families, stepfamilies, and children who no longer live with either birth parent but with adoptive or foster parents."[56]

These figures based on racial and ethnic groups add even more insight. For example, "54% of white youth live with both married parents; 41% of teenagers from multiracial family backgrounds live in intact families; 40% of hispanic teenagers nationwide live with both parents; and 17% of african-american youth live with both married parents."[57]

Robert Rector references the correlation of family structure and childhood poverty across racial and ethnic lines:

> Marriage is associated with lower rates of poverty separately for whites, blacks, and hispanics. Within each racial and ethnic group, the poverty rate for married couples is substantially lower than the poverty rate for non-married families of the same race or ethnicity.

- Among non-hispanic white married couples, the poverty rate was 3.2 percent, while the rate for non-married white families was seven times higher at 22.0 percent.
- Among hispanic married families, the poverty rate was 13.2 percent, while the poverty rate among non-married families was three times higher at 37.9 percent.

[56] Ibid.
[57] Ibid.

- Among black married couples, the poverty rate was 7.0 percent, while the rate for non-married black families was greater than five times higher at 35.6 percent.[58]

Marriage is a sound vehicle to preserve economic mobility for all citizens. Our country can only be as strong as its citizens, and a dearth of strong families weakens the human, societal, and ethical character of the United States. Fragile families can create a vulnerable, anemic nation. Our country will not be able to maintain its leadership role unless parents establish a firm leadership role in their communities.

"We must to a better job of educating people. Young people and parents alike typically believe, regardless of background or life experience, that their chances of divorcing are 50 percent. They do not know that their chances of divorce decrease if their parents are still married, they graduate from college, they do not have a child before marrying, they do not cohabitate before marriage, they are not poor, they have the same religious values, and they participate in premarital preparation."[59]

How can we remedy the cultural rash of parental rejection that challenges the growth and success of youth across America? The first step is to understand and acknowledge that we have a serious problem that affects every community in the nation. Next, we can communicate with neighbors, educators, community leaders, and ambassadors within houses of worship on the central matter.[60] We need to ensure that strategies and tactics are defined and implemented, and then we can follow up and evaluate progress.

---

[58] https://www.heritage.org/poverty-and-inequality/report/marriage-americas-greatest-weapon-against-child-poverty. For additional information on US Census data (2014) linked to children living with two parents into adulthood across the educational and racial spectrum, see https://ifstudies.org/blog/more-than-60-of-u-s-kids-live-with-two-biological-parents.

[59] https://medium.com/2016-index-of-culture-and-opportunity/divorce-in-our-nation-b2f69db56872.

[60] Each community leader plays a role in communicating the need to support the development of the children they lead. Each mentor plays an independent role in broadcasting the need. Each takes action independently.

We can stimulate action by working with local leaders and learn what approaches are leveraged today to address the underlying cause of the degradation of America's youth. Become aware of the strategies that encompass enhanced education, community awareness, and social reform. We may not have all the answers, but we can put suggestions in play to help stimulate a tipping point of cultural change toward uplifting the youth of America through a commitment of responsible parental attachment.

To create a cultural revival for our young, we need to be proactive and creative, and the efforts need to come from every facet of society. The first and most crucial step is to trigger an "It Takes Two" movement that decries parental avoidance and values an intact household above all else. Then we must teach people how to communicate, manage conflict, and regulate their emotions to create a loving, nurturing environment in which children can thrive.

On a broader level, we can recruit help from the media by developing major campaigns that are broadcast regularly on the need for change and parental guidance. Similarly, the sports and entertainment industry can serve to create a cultural renewal that supports and promotes intact families. To this end, an advertising program can be developed that addresses family unity. Reality shows can center on children living in broken homes across America. Bring forward movies, music, documentaries, or a TV series to imprint the decay of intact American families and the associated outcomes. Educational funds can be allocated in each state to raise awareness and teach students about the value of intact families. Students could earn course credit for participation in early childhood and family-learning programs. High schools, colleges, and universities could enhance their curriculum by including courses specific to the social science of preserving the culture of the American family, and we can restore an emphasis on vocational or trade programs as extensions to the curriculum for high schools to support student employment.

Going even further, here are a few more tasks that are needed to solve this cultural crisis:

- Require community leaders to address parental responsibility in all district schools.
- Raise awareness of parental obligations and denounce parental detachment in community houses of worship.
- Members of broken homes who experienced hardships from not having an intact family can address students within communities.
- Pressure politicians and lawmakers to revise laws that inflame social dependence, and pronounce the requirement for parental belonging.

These are simply a few suggestions, and they may not be novel, but they can stimulate dialogue and a movement to change. Convening a roundtable in every community, county, or state that includes informed and experienced people in the areas of social science, parental guidance, childhood development, education, spiritual renewal, entertainment, sports, media and communications, political advocacy, and others can serve as a springboard to elucidate solutions that create action for restoring a family-based culture. Such an approach can only progress if leaders within our communities choose to lead and recognize the need to change.

On the educational front, city and state chancellors, administrators, and directors charged with the responsibility for educating and developing the youth they serve need to carefully review their performance outcomes, relative to state and national standards. They can strategically consider reallocating funds for educational programs that address social responsibility through parenting and family values.

As example, "for the 2017–2018 schoolyear NYC's Department of Educational Operating Budget was 24.3 Billion dollars for traditional educational costs."[61] That's $24.3 billion for one year, and the amount disbursed over the past five years has been relatively the same. That totals over $121 billion over the past half-decade. And when correlating the expenditures for the past five years with the performance achieved

---

[61] https://schools.nyc.gov.

in the New York City Graduation and Readiness for College rates, the results are well below the New York State averages. Even though there has been a slight improvement over the past couple of years, "the five-year average (2013–2017) reflects a 67% graduation rate according to the NY State method."[62]

And the rates referenced are skewed by a portion of the New York City schools that are performing well above the average. Additionally, the "Readiness for College rate for the same time period was 52%."[63]

As taxpayers funding the city, state, and federal contributions for the Department of Education, we need to understand the outcomes and value of the educational support our children receive. Currently, the performance reflects a high proportion of students who are ill-equipped and ill-prepared for college or workplace entry. As a result, we need to consider the burden of not having children advance in the educational system or workplace. One potential consequence of weak educational performance includes a generation of adolescents who struggle to find their way in communities across New York City. Such an outcome is not acceptable. The cycle of educational mediocrity requires interruption, with a renewed focus to create change and to drive improved performance.

Additionally, the New York City Department of Education outlines the following in its 2017–2018 Budgets and Fair School Funding report:

"The Formula for Funding Is Strongly Aligned to the Framework for Great Schools. The funding model provides a student achievement centered approach to funding schools. Transparency in the formula increases trust and supports *strong family-community ties."*[64]

The families referenced in their formula are, in many cases, not intact. So the DOE is attempting to build trust within communities that, for the past fifty years, have recognized a rapid erosion of the family unit. Therefore, the formula is flawed and needs reconstruction.

---

[62] Ibid.

[63] Ibid.

[64] https://www.nycenet.edu/offices/finance_schools/budget/DSBPO/allocationmemo/fy18_19/FY19_docs/FY2019_FSF_Guide.pdf.

Greater education on the requirement for understanding the social obligation of parenting, personal responsibility, and educational value is a platform that needs to be incorporated in *every* school very early in childhood education.

My wife and I understand how difficult single parenting must be, as does any married person with children. Having two parents involved, the responsibility is daunting, and even with the noblest efforts, aberrations may surface. And any single parent who can raise a child to become a capable, socially responsible, and productive adult should be extremely proud of his or her accomplishment. The independent responsibility of providing a wide range of support to a child is a significant undertaking, and being a sole provider means having to shoulder an enormous load in every developmental category.

As noted, millions of children in the US are living and learning in an environment where their parents have divorced. With optimal supervision, commitment, and dedication from each parent, there is the potential for greatness in children who come from broken homes. I am sure there are numerous examples of individuals who were raised by displaced parents and became highly successful and productive adults. This requires continuous coordination by both parents, and each parent independently must play an active role in the child's development. Coordination, integration, and involvement are essential.

My brother and my sister both were divorced and had multiple children. In each instance, their children received proportionate care and guidance; they acclimated to their circumstances and went on to build sound careers. I also have close friends who have been divorced for several years and work cooperatively with their ex-spouses to ensure their children receive all the support they deserve. Their youngsters have adapted quite remarkably and have developed into confident and determined young adults.

Unfortunately, there are children within our communities who may not receive the required parental care to support their development. Youth within single-parent homes may endure hardships that result from financial strains. As example, single parents having less available income may preclude or limit the availability of resources to complement childhood development. Having additional resources to support single parents could help bolster social skills through involvement in after-school programs for participating youth. Ultimately, the availability of supportive programs would serve as an important parental adjunct to enhance the well-being of the young.

It seems clear that a child who is raised in a two-parent home will have the potential to achieve and capitalize on available opportunities. What chronic triggers exist that create a wedge and erode parental unions? For over fifty years, we have seen the same trend continue, with children enduring the challenge of being raised by single parents. Should this societal tendency continue and should Americans choose to look the other way, the prospects for a vibrant future of productive citizens is not favorable. Children living in these households are bound to face challenges that youngsters in nuclear families may not.

Leading change to build up the youth of America is a tall order, but we can all assist in leading by being part of the solution. We can start by *regenerating the strength of the American family* and guide our children willingly. I was privileged to grow up in a challenged low-income neighborhood with great leaders, starting with my parents. Our community leaders wanted to develop children to be productive, responsible adults. They wanted to provide education and social support to frame the characters of the youth within the neighborhood. They wanted to build up their young to understand the value of respect for self and others and grow into loving adults. They wanted us to achieve. We had leaders who cared and wanted to make a difference.

Additionally, I was fortunate to spend thirty years in the pharmaceutical business, with over 75 percent of my career cast in leadership roles. I recognize the clear parallels in the culture of business and the culture of parenting and leading children to achieve. For example, when senior management fails to establish a strong sense of urgency to achieve objectives and forecasts, productivity wanes. It's hard to move people out of their comfort zones. In the absence of urgency, people will not give you additional effort that is required to consistently achieve favorable outcomes. They hold on to the status quo, and company performance suffers—and so does shareholder value.

John P. Kotter, a foremost expert on business leadership, notes in his book, *Leading Change*, "By far the biggest mistake people make when trying to change organizations is to plunge ahead without establishing a high enough sense of urgency in fellow managers and employees. This error is fatal because transformations always fail to achieve their objectives when complacency levels are high."[65]

In similar fashion, what we witness in our society today is a culture stalled in the status quo regarding the ultimate responsibility of parental guidance in childhood development. Having two parents actively engaged in the development of their children is well below standard. In using the overwhelming data and studies on childhood belonging as a reflection of parental performance, a strong sense of urgency is required to course correct and provide children with the leadership they need so they can achieve. Children who do not receive leadership strength during their formative years may find it difficult to grow into confident and capable adults.

A parental leadership gap exists within our communities, and complacency is at the core. With no sense of urgency, with an anemic leadership that fails to recognize that change is required, without a guiding team established, and without vision, it is no wonder we have been stuck in the mire for the past half century. We have simply accepted tarnished parental values and support for childhood development. Major change is required, and unless community leaders establish a vision, appoint a guiding coalition, and broadcast that vision to the masses, it will be hard to appeal to the minds and actions of people in our society.

John Kotter outlines a specific process for creating major change. In my view, his action plans align with the requirements for implanting cultural change in parental responsibility and childhood development. He indicates that while many of us still have a lot to learn, there

---

[65] John P. Kotter, *Leading Change* (Harvard Business Press, 1996), 4.

are two components to understanding the transformation: "The first relates to the various steps in the staged process for creating major change," whereas the second is about *"leadership, leadership, and still more leadership."*[66]

The process Kotter highlights for creating major change has several steps: "Establishing a sense of urgency, creating the guiding coalition, developing a vision and strategy, communicating the change vision, empowering a broad base of people to take action, generating short-term wins, consolidating gains and producing even more change, and institutionalizing new approaches in the culture."[67] He clarifies that the first few steps help break down the status quo, the middle steps bring in new ways to shape society, "and the last stage grounds the changes in the culture and makes them stick."[68]

Such an approach to creating major change to build strength in America's youth may seem too algorithmic. My intention, however, is to reference and build upon tried-and-true methods for creating change within our culture; any array of approaches is worth defining and implementing. This is particularly relevant and vital as it relates to establishing a parental culture that values childhood development.

There is another simple approach, which is to do nothing and follow the same futile path of status quo that leads to further degradation of the family unit and results in children who are challenged to compete; many are fixed in desolation and disillusionment. Stay the course, and you choose to further erode the security, intellect, and personal growth within our country. Stagnate, and you choose to invite our youth into passages of weak education, violence, poverty, denial of law and order, drug usage, and social dependence … just to name a few consequences of doing nothing.

The spirit of the human condition can overcome any negative force or ill will. We have advanced our national intellect and capacity to achieve in every way since our nation was formed. To simply

---

[66] Ibid., 31

[67] Ibid., 20–22.

[68] Ibid.

leave parenting as a personal elective is to remove responsibility and advancement of the human condition. Our nation demands and requires childhood development by willing parents. We must choose to change and to reject the status quo.

Spark a change—and lead! Follow a pathway that elucidates the value of parental belonging. It's the preferred peaceful choice and the right choice for all. We all need to break out of the bonds of complacency and boldly move toward the future. Accepting the status quo as it relates to the development and well-being of America's youth will hinder the creation of our future entrepreneurs and leaders.

The Leadership Secrets of Colin Powell by Oren Harari highlights character as an essential element of leading people.

> Leaders with character *stand for something*—a value, an ideal, a cause, a mission. Moreover, leaders with character don't just talk about these things. They exhibit a coherent pattern of behavior that demonstrates what they stand for. In Powell's words, they "figure out what is crucial," and they "stay focused on it," without allowing side issues to distract them.[69]

Colin Powell, born and raised in the Bronx, honed his leadership skills early on, positioning him favorably as a distinguished principal in the military and political arenas. We can all take a cue from Powell and stand for something valuable … and lead our youth on a mission to succeed.

Changing our lethargic ways in parenting requires a clear vision and strategy on how to progress. This outline is meant to stimulate a thought process, a simple pathway to assist you in helping to guide and support the youth you want to inspire. And to create meaningful change, we need to be confident, committed, and knowledgeable. We can break away from fear, habit, and comfort; we can look to the future

---

[69] Oren Harari, *The Leadership Secrets of Colin Powell* (McGraw Hill, 2002), 204.

and reengineer a movement toward developing capable youth. Those individuals courageous enough to embrace a new beginning and lead will provide a critical service for the children in our communities. There is no greater reward than motivating and coaching children to become peaceful, loving, and successful adults. In the end, we all win.

SUMMARY

Having two loving parents to depend upon from childhood to adulthood is a blessing, one that must be preserved and shared. All children deserve to be aligned with caring parents who guide, protect, and encourage their young to achieve. More directly, it is our responsibility as adults to foster and promote the need to raise children within an intact family, one filled with core values that reflect respect for others. There is no greater reward for humanity than building up our youth under a flag of respect, pride, and desire to achieve.

Living in a low-income Bronx housing project with two parents and four siblings during the '60s and '70s provided a ripe haven for learning about people, willingness to sacrifice, and the importance of unwavering parental love. Our parents provided a secure foundation for us to embrace. We were eager to experience the life that surrounded us, and in the process, we developed important skills that helped us capably navigate challenges, seek opportunities, and build solid careers.

Any success that I have earned is a result of the tangible childhood learning from my family, faith, education, mentors, friends, and environment. I was fortunate to have parents and others around me to provide guidance, instruction, motivation, and nurturing. These essential elements prepared and helped me build the confidence and drive to achieve. Having a family unit with resident values anchored me—and countless others—with a raw desire to advance and become self-sufficient. I learned to avoid violence and reject racism, and I framed every encounter with a spirit of respect for others.

In many cases, children growing up in the absence of nuclear families are less inclined to learn similar values, and many falter and fall victim to poverty, rejection, disarray, and a cycle of dependence. As a community, we need to center our efforts on the ultimate value of having two parents who are committed to building strength in the children they lead. This cornerstone is the key to rebuilding trust and respect among people. Having two parents guiding the young is a reasonable, holistic solution to help curb our growing societal troubles. We can no longer become absorbed in the symptoms of parental avoidance; rather, we can reverse such negative communal trends and energetically broadcast the obvious and favorable benefits of living within a stable family unit.

Anyone who is responsible for directing the care of our young into adulthood has good reason to embrace the logic outlined in this guide. As guardians of the children we lead, we can bring forward the spiritual justice required to ensure our youth achieve. We are a community of shepherds, accountable for the development and well-being of the young we serve. Modeling the way with integrity and relentless dedication will help build character and strength in the youth across America. Societal unification depends on parental leadership, and we, as parents are the arbiters of harmony in the communities of America. We are all lucky to have a life to live. We can all choose to bring forward good will toward others. We can all seek unity through mentoring and leading our young. Parental unity coupled with spiritual devotion will yield loving children capable of learning and delivering favorable outcomes independently. Make the choice for what is right.

IT TAKES TWO

Thinking about how our children have grown over the years, I ask the same question that most parents do: where has the time gone? Yes, it does go by in a blink. Today, Susan and I still convene with our children over meals to discuss the issues of the day and how they are progressing in their endeavors. I cut back on the meatloaf for breakfast, but I enjoy our family time nonetheless. Over the past two decades, we have had the good fortune of recognizing the diversity of talents, behaviors, and aspirations of our children. We have been involved in every aspect of their lives since birth, and it is beyond fulfilling to see how they have developed into capable, peaceful young adults.

Daniel, as the eldest child, is the cerebral guardian who makes every effort to succeed in his endeavors. He embodies spiritual strength, carries confidence into his daily activities, and is committed to his family in every way. He possesses a strong drive to achieve and respects others willingly. Amy, our middle child, makes every effort to understand behaviors and embraces good will. She is more cautious in her approach and shows a consistent drive to learn and achieve goals. She is devoted to finding peace through helping others and is seeking a career that supports the growth of those with special needs. Emily, as the youngest of our tribe, is always confident and comfortable in her decisions and actions. She has learned to listen to and observe those around her and is independently capable of forming strategies and solutions to succeed. She is not hesitant to embrace newness and seeks to enjoy each day with self-assurance.

And my wife, Susan, is the anchor of our family. She continues to bring forward endless strength, patience, and love to each of us. She is a selfless giver and finds joy in seeing others at peace. For more than two decades, she has assisted in the religious education of the young and remains focused on spiritual development.

I have had the great pleasure of witnessing everyone in my family continuing to grow and develop as loving adults, eager to achieve and determined to bring joy and peace to those they encounter. I am blessed and look forward to sharing life lessons with each of them in the same fashion that I have since 1989.

APPENDIX

Health Care Costs and the
Pharmaceutical Industry

Having spent over thirty years in the pharmaceutical industry, I feel inclined to provide commentary and insight into the value of the industry and the associated costs for pharmaceuticals, relative to the overall national health care expenditures.

From my perspective, the advancement of pharmaceuticals in the health care arena is significantly downplayed, considering the vast contribution to improved health outcomes and increased life expectancy. People live much longer today, as compared to the '60s; some factors include advanced specialty medicine, medical technology, clinical research, and hospital and pharmaceutical care. There should be a heightened appreciation and gratitude toward the pharmaceutical industry, just as there is for specialty physicians and teaching hospitals.

I completely agree that the industry must be mindful and vigilant of the costs of pharmaceuticals and maintain reasonable pricing practices across all product categories. People need medicine to help ameliorate and eradicate disease and should not be short-changed on life expectancy because they cannot afford valuable medications. As a point of reference, most "adults over the age of 65 are on 4 to 5 medications"[70]

---

[70] NCHS, National Health and Nutrition Examination Survey (NHANES), http://www.cdc.gov/nchs/hus/contents2016.htm#fig15.

to curb various diseases, and their life expectancies have dramatically increased. "During 1975–2015, life expectancy increased from 68.8 to 76.3 for males and from 76.6 to 81.2 for females."[71] Additionally, these same individuals who consumed multiple medications had decreased hospital visits as a result of advances in the development of pharmaceuticals. Examples include but are not limited to the usage of medications to treat asthma, elevated cholesterol, COPD, severe infections, depression/anxiety, GI disorders, and hypertension. Pharmaceutical treatment can reduce hospital stays, which reduces the overall cost of care. Therefore, when people are living longer because of improved care and increased pharmaceutical usage, the associated cost of pharmaceuticals will grow proportionately.

The pharmaceutical arena gets a black eye when the national health care budget is evaluated. Take a closer look at the costs for each bucket within the health care budget, and you will recognize that one area that needs increased scrutiny is hospital costs. When a patient is admitted into a hospital for treatment of a specific illness, there is a sequence of costs that requires greater analysis and evaluation of what is reasonable and customary.

Look at the National Health Care Expenditures for 2010 and 2015. You will see the absolute expenditures for prescription drugs had a negligible percentage increase relative to the overall health care costs, and growth increased by 25 percent. For hospital care, there was a slight percentage increase and 40 percent growth over the five-year period. You can ascertain a realistic trend when you look over time, as opposed to looking narrowly, year over year.

Pharma companies need to continue to boldly pursue the development of novel compounds that improve the quality of life for people around the globe. At the same time, once a new product is launched, the cost to the patient should be top of mind to ensure affordability and consistency of use. We have a great health care system in the US, and all the services provided contribute to improving health outcomes. We are the beneficiaries of the collective services offered,

---

[71] http://www.cdc.gov/nchs/hus/contents2016.htm#fig06.

and that comes at a price. The price we pay yields extraordinary dividends in enhancing the quality and duration life.

The next time you hear someone within any corridor chirp about the cost of pharmaceuticals, you can enlighten them and let them know the pharmaceutical industry contributes mightily to preserving and extending life. These are the facts; you can draw your own conclusions.

2010 National Health Expenditures (in Billions)

Appendix Charts

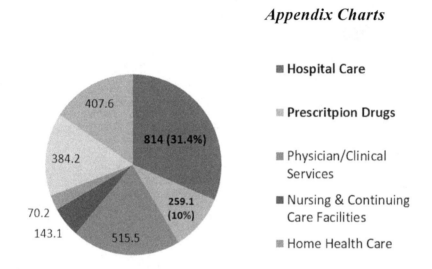

- Hospital Care
- Prescritpion Drugs
- Physician/Clinical Services
- Nursing & Continuing Care Facilities
- Home Health Care

In 2010, national health expenditures for prescription drugs accounted for 10 percent of the overall budget at $259.1 billion, compared to hospital care, representing 31.4 percent of the budget at $814 billion.[72]

---

[72] Kaiser Family Foundation calculations using NHE data from Center for Medicare and Medicaid Services, Office of the Actuary, National Health Statistics Group. http://www.cms.hhs.gov/NationalHealthExpendData/.

2015 National Health Expenditures (in Billions)

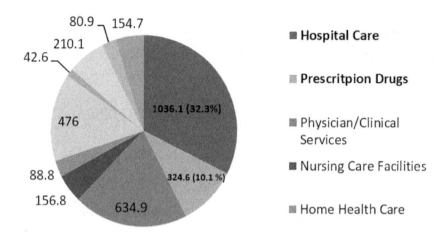

In 2015, national health expenditures for prescription drugs accounted for 10.1 percent of the overall budget at $324.6 billion, compared to hospital care, representing 32.3 percent of the budget and $1,036.1 billion.[73]

---

[73] Center for Medicare and Medicaid Services, Office of the Actuary, National Health Statistics Group, National Health Expenditure Accounts, National Health Expenditures. https://www.cms.gov/Research-Statistics-Data-and-Systems/Statistics-Trends-and Reports/NationalHealthExpendData/NationalHealthAccountsHistorical.html (accessed January 5, 2017).

PHOTOGRAPHIC MEMORIES

Dad 1945   Mom 1945

Mom and Dad with Uncle Walter and Aunt Faye
on their Wedding Day- May 5th 1951

TEAM AZZARI

Nancy   Gary

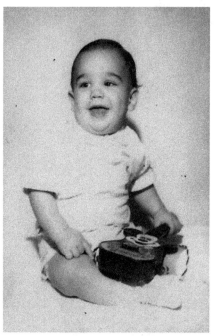

Gregory   Geoffrey

Gerard

THE NEIGHBORHOOD

Immaculate Conception Church and School-
Gun Hill Road- Bronx, New York

Gun Hill Projects...across from the Church

Home…3445 Holland Avenue

Gun Hill Playground…across from the Projects…
the site for many spirited games

Second Grade

Immaculate Conception School- Bronx, New York

Evander Childs High School- Gun Hill Road- Bronx, New York

The #2 Train Station...on the western side of the
Projects on Gun Hill and White Plains Roads

Alexander's Department Store- Fordham Road and Grand Concourse

United States Post Office-Grand Concourse and 149th Street

Yankee Stadium-Bronx, NY

Saint Raymond's High School- Bronx, New York

Fordham University- Keating Hall- Bronx, New York

Old Fordham Ram Meets the New...Tradition Remains the Same

Riverdale Neighborhood House- Bronx, New York

M&R Deli, Mount Kisco, NY...place for tasty *meatloaf for breakfast*

The 4 Gs with Mom...looks like the 80s

Greg and I with Mom- Niece Christine's wedding, 2004

La Famiglia- Mom's 65th birthday party, 1992

Mom at Cabrini Nursing Home, 2004

Leading the Forest Sales Team

Forest partners...Mark, Arnie, Jerry, and Cary

4Gs

With Dom 'Beepo' and Rocco of River's Edge

Gary and Greg with childhood frends Henry and John

A few Immaculate peers gather over 50 years later…
Chris, Mike, Carmine and Colin, 2017

Champion foursome at a St. Ray's Golf
outing with a few Raven cronies...

Henry, John and Bill, 2017

St. Ray's Varsity Basketball Team, 1978

1995 Four Gs champion softball team

LOCAL PORTALS

River's Edge Restaurant-Yonkers, NY

Bridges- Bronx, NY

B&Bs- Pelham, NY

Chatterbox 54- Briarcliff Manor, NY

LITTLE ITALY...THE BRONX

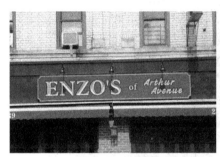

Fordham University in the shadows of Little Italy

REGENERATION

A Galvanized American Spirit

Some favorite songs of the '60s and '70s that may ring a bell are referenced below.

Thanks to *PasteMagazine.com* for helping assemble these hits based on feedback from their voters. The songs are in no particular order. I like them all. If you are not fond of these hits, then feel free to gather your favorite tunes and listen to those.

The 1960s were considered the best decade for music in America. I guess that depends upon your taste. The British Invasion was an awakening, and along with the blues, rock, pop, and jazz, a new genre was thrust on the scene.

Great Songs of the '60s

- Frank Sinatra, "My Way"
- The Monkees, "I'm a Believer"
- The Beach Boys, "God Only Knows"
- Ben E. King, "Stand by Me"
- Neil Diamond, "Sweet Caroline"
- Jackie Wilson, "(Your Love Keeps Lifting Me) Higher and Higher"
- Bobby Darin, "Beyond the Sea"
- The Righteous Brothers, "Unchained Melody"
- The Crystals, "Then He Kissed Me"
- The Marvelettes, "Please Mr. Postman"
- The Four Tops, "Bernadette"
- Beach Boys, "Good Vibrations"
- Frankie Valli and the Four Seasons, "Can't Take My Eyes Off of You"
- Wilson Pickett, "Mustang Sally"
- Edwin Starr, "War"
- Dusty Springfield, "Son of a Preacher Man"
- Led Zeppelin, "Dazed and Confused"
- The Shangri-Las, "Leader of the Pack"
- Louis Armstrong, "What a Wonderful World"
- The Hollies, "Bus Stop"
- James Brown, "Papa's Got a Brand-New Bag"
- The Shirelles, "Will You Love Me Tomorrow?"

- The Zombies, "She's Not There"
- The Troggs, "Wild Thing"
- Smokey Robinson, "Tears of a Clown"
- The Yardbirds, "For Your Love"
- Tommy James and the Shondells, "Crimson and Clover"
- Patsy Cline, "Crazy"
- Bob Dylan, "Blowin' in the Wind"
- The Beatles, "I Want to Hold Your Hand"
- Sly & the Family Stone, "Everyday People"
- Etta James, "At Last"
- Marvin Gaye and Tammi Terrell, "Ain't No Mountain High Enough"
- Johnny Cash, "Ring of Fire"
- The Rolling Stones, "(I Can't Get No) Satisfaction"
- Van Morrison, "Brown-Eyed Girl"
- The Animals, "House of the Rising Sun"
- The Doors, "Light My Fire"
- The Temptations, "My Girl"
- The Zombies, "Time of the Season"
- Jimi Hendrix, "Purple Haze"
- Jefferson Airplane, "White Rabbit"
- Otis Redding, "(Sittin' on) The Dock of the Bay"
- The Who, "My Generation"
- The Band, "The Weight"
- The Turtles, "Happy Together"
- Simon & Garfunkel, "The Sounds of Silence"
- Sam Cooke, "A Change Is Gonna Come"
- Steppenwolf, "Born to be Wild"
- Bob Dylan, "Like a Rolling Stone"
- The Mamas & the Papas, "California Dreamin'"

Following the '60s and the era of cultural change, the '70s brought together a wide variety of music. As listeners, we had numerous choices, and many bands shot up at different points in the decade. Music of the time included rock, hard rock (head-banging music), funk, soul, R&B, pop, soft rock, disco, reggae, and the on-boarding of hip-hop.

Thanks to *superseventies.com* for helping assemble these hits. The songs are in no particular order.

Great Songs of the '70s

- Simon & Garfunkel, "Bridge Over Troubled Water"
- The Guess Who, "American Woman"
- The Jackson Five, "ABC"
- The Beatles, "Let It Be"
- Three Dog Night, "Mama Told Me Not to Come"
- Three Dog Night, "Joy to the World"
- Carole King, "It's Too Late"
- The Bee Gees, "How Can You Mend a Broken Heart"
- The Temptations, "Just My Imagination"
- Don McLean, "American Pie"
- Looking Glass, "Brandy"
- Bill Withers, "Lean on Me"
- Jim Croce, "Bad, Bad Leroy Brown"
- Paul McCartney & Wings, "My Love"
- Marvin Gaye, "Let's Get It On"
- Billy Paul, "Me and Mrs. Jones"
- Barbra Streisand, "The Way We Were"
- Redbone, "Come and Get Your Love"
- Al Wilson, "Show and Tell"
- Grand Funk Railroad, "The Loco-Motion"
- Elton John, "Bennie and the Jets"
- David Bowie, "Fame"
- Earth, Wind & Fire, "Shining Star"
- Eagles, "One of These Nights"
- Average White Band, "Pick Up the Pieces"
- Johnnie Taylor, "Disco Lady"
- Wild Cherry, "Play That Funky Music"
- Rod Stewart, "Tonight's the Night"
- Manhattans, "Kiss and Say Goodbye"
- The Four Seasons, "December 1963 (Oh, What a Night)"

- Barbra Streisand, "Evergreen"
- Abba, "Dancing Queen"
- Rita Coolidge, "Higher and Higher"
- Bee Gees, "Saturday Night Fever"
- Bee Gees, "Stayin' Alive"
- Commodores, "Three Times a Lady"
- A Taste of Honey, "Boogie Oogie"
- Player, "Baby Come Back"
- The Knack, "My Sharona"
- Chic, "Le Freak"
- Donna Summer, "Bad Girls"
- Anita Ward, "Ring My Bell"
- Donna Summer, "Hot Stuff"
- Bee Gees, "Too Much Heaven"
- Fleetwood Mac, "Over My Head"
- The Rolling Stones, "Angie"
- Styx, "Babe"
- The O'Jays, "Backstabbers"
- The Temptations, "Ball of Confusion"
- The Doobie Brothers, "Black Water"
- Bruce Springsteen, "Born to Run"
- The Rolling Stones, "Brown Sugar"
- Sammy Davis Jr., "The Candy Man"
- Harry Chapin, "Cat's in the Cradle"
- King Harvest, "Dancing in the Moonlight"
- Badfinger, "Day After Day"
- Fleetwood Mac, "Dreams"
- Dobie Gray, "Drift Away"
- Ray Stevens, "Everything Is Beautiful"
- Sly and the Family Stone, "Family Affair"
- Ohio Players, "Fire"
- The Edgar Winter Group, "Frankenstein"
- George Harrison, "Give Me Love"
- Bill Conti, "Gonna Fly Now"
- Michael Jackson, "Got to Be There"
- Blue Swede, "Hooked on a Feeling"
- America, "Horse with No Name"

- Eagles, "Hotel California"
- Neil Diamond, "I Am, I Said"
- Eric Clapton, "I Shot the Sheriff"
- The Jackson Five, "I'll Be There"
- Chicago, "If You Leave Me Now"
- Ringo Starr, "It Don't Come Easy"
- The Beatles, "The Long and Winding Road"
- The O'Jays, "Love Train"
- George Harrison, "My Sweet Lord"
- Bob Seger, "Night Moves"
- Billy Preston, "Nothing from Nothing"
- The Chi-Lites, "Oh Girl"
- The Temptations, "Papa Was s Rollin' Stone"
- Ringo Starr, "Photograph"
- Alice Cooper, "School's Out"
- Gordon Lightfoot, "Sundown"
- Aerosmith, "Sweet Emotion"
- The Grass Roots, "Temptation Eyes"
- Marvin Gaye, "What's Going On?"

Great Movies of the '60s and '70s

The counterculture of the '60s influenced Hollywood to produce movies by taking more chances. The decade of the 1970s began weakly, with the industry facing a financial and artistic gap, but eventually the decade became a creative high point in the US film industry. As a result of the freedom movement in the '60s, there were fewer restrictions on language, violence, and adult content. The hippie and civil rights movements, the peace-and-love theme, exploration with drugs, and the growth of rock and roll clearly had an impact. Hollywood was renewed with a swell of novel movies that aligned to the culture of the time.

Some of my favorites of the era were industry classics that still resonate today, and when I see them on cable TV, I stop and recall great memories of days gone by. Movies that sparked my interest are referenced below in no particular order:

- The Godfather, 1972
- Jaws, 1975
- Psycho, 1960
- Rocky, 1976
- The Birds, 1963
- A Clockwork Orange, 1971
- Bonnie and Clyde, 1967
- The Dirty Dozen, 1967
- Lawrence of Arabia, 1962
- The Exorcist, 1973
- Blazing Saddles, 1974
- Cool Hand Luke, 1967
- The Godfather: Part II, 1974
- Taxi Driver,1976
- The Great Escape, 1963
- 2001: A Space Odyssey, 1968
- Apocalypse Now, 1978
- Cleopatra, 1963
- Young Frankenstein, 1974
- Dr. No, 1962
- Sisters, 1972
- Easy Rider, 1969
- Carrie, 1976
- Paper Moon, 1973
- Lord of the Flies, 1963
- The Goodbye Girl, 1977
- The Graduate, 1967
- The Hustler, 1961
- Sleuth, 1972
- A Fistful of Dollars, 1964
- Kramer vs. Kramer, 1979
- Guess Who's Coming to Dinner?, 1967
- All the President's Men, 1976
- The Omen, 1976
- Night of the Living Dead, 1968
- In the Heat of the Night, 1967
- Patton, 1970
- Planet of the Apes, 1968
- Dog Day Afternoon, 1975
- The Good, the Bad and the Ugly, 1966
- Murderers' Row, 1966
- Spartacus, 1960
- Goldfinger, 1964
- Bullitt, 1968
- The Manchurian Candidate, 1962
- Funny Girl, 1968
- One Flew Over the Cuckoo's Nest, 1975
- Deliverance, 1972
- Papillon, 1973
- Escape from Alcatraz, 1979
- Close Encounters of the Third Kind, 1977
- El Dorado, 1966
- Hard Times, 1975

Gun Hill Projects Family Members and Their Occupations*

Anthony Ceritelli—Packaging, Business Development Mgr.

Anthony Polizzi—Owner, Taxi/School Bus Service

Anthony Sweeney—Lawyer/ Education

Artie Rastelli—Carpet Distribution

Barbara Candela—Health Care

Barbara Luciano—Nursing

Bill O'Sullivan—Education/ Coach

Bill Perry—Gasoline Industry, Sales Director

Billy Martinetti—NYC Sanitation

Bob Conroy—United Federation of Teachers

Bob Fonsecca—IBM/Musician

Bob Moran—Restaurant Manager/Bartender

Bob Piano—Education/ Basketball Coach

Brian Corby—Reinsurance Claims Executive

Brian Spears—Education/ Basketball Coach

Carl "Raw Talent" Wright—Lithography

Chris Scandiffio—Real Estate, Sales

Craig Munson—Owner, Copy Center

Dennis Conroy—CEO/ Communications Consultant

Dom Tana—Social Service/ Restaurateur

Ed D'Erasmo—Metro Transportation Authority

Ed Sanders—US Postal Service

Eileen Licata—Human Resources/Benefits

Fran Bartko—Clothing Merchandiser/Hallmark Displays

Frank George—NYC Fireman

Frank Hughes—Teacher/ Educational Sales

Frank Licata—Technologies Director

Frank Mason—Artist/Painter

Fred Hirt—Information and Technology

Gary Azzari—Telecommunications

Geoffrey Azzari—Education/ Football Coach

Gerard Azzari—Pharmaceutical Sales

Gregory Azzari—US Postal Service

Harry Clancy—Stockbroker/ Mortgage Broker

Henry Lopez—Information and Technology, Owner

Italo Valentini—Information and Technology

Jack Curcuruto—Importer/ Wholesaler, Apparel

Jack Renzulli—Mechanics/Tools

James Marino—Verizon, Installer

Jane Campisi—Education, Principal

Jane Grasso—Education, Principal

Janet Spears—Education, Principal

Jerry Cuomo—Office Installations, Owner

Jim Harris—Education, Principal

Joe Candela—Ironworker

Joe Cuomo—Electrical Contractor

Joe DeFrancis—Con Edison, Manager

Joe Gagliano—NYC Police Department

Joe Kiely—International/ Domestic Transportation

Joe Mitchell—Jostens, Sales

Joe Morretti—Pops Bar, Owner

John Fino   Elevator Mechanic/ Inspector

John Hopkins—Manufacturing/ Transportation

John Hungreter—United Parcel Service

John Kennedy—Insurance

John Luciano—Electrical Contractor

John Mascaro—Mechanical Engineer/Oil & Gas

John Ragucci—Credit Manager

John Santoianni—US Postal Service

Kevin Moran—Book Editor

Larry "Lightbulb" Thomas— Four Gs Musician

Louie Mongello—Con Edison

Lou Cubello—Restauranteur

Marie Tibaldi—Education

Mario Giordano—Toyota Dealership, Managing Director

Martin Kauffman—Social Worker

Mike DeStephano—United Parcel Service

Mike Dimerco—NYPD

Mike Kiely—Automotive Industry, Service Director

Mike LaFiandra—Consumer Goods, Sales

Mike Miraglia—Actuary

Mike Rendine—Elvis Impersonator

Milty Walzer—Education

Neil Moran—United Parcel Service

Nick Salzano—Owner, Plumbing Supplies

Paul Pellino—Veterans Administration

Aileen Pellino—Nurse

Phil Maniaci—American Airlines, Cargo

Phil Vasquez—NYC Fireman

Philip Sherman—Physician

Ralph Candela—Physician

Randall Hirt—Telecommunications

Ray Crosby—Information and Technology, VP

Richard Mamano—NYPD/ Private Investigator

Richard Nunez—Lawyer

Richie Holz—Tiffany & Company, Sales

Richie Kupermintz—Dog Trainer

Rico Jamonte—Education

Robert Ciccarone—Department of Corrections

Robert Detiberiis—Heavy Construction, Supervisor

Robert Marra—Television Advertising Executive

Robert McNiff—Nestles Corporation, Sales

Robert Ricciardi—Electrician

Robert Schulze— Telecommunications

Robert Terranova—Chemical Engineer

Rocco Scarcella—Education/ Restauranteur

Ron Delucia—Metro Transportation Authority

Rosalie Deangelis—Nursing

Roy Sico—Transit Police Department/NY State Courts

Scott Hungreter—NYC Police Department

Steve Strain—Government Service

Stephen Mangione—Public Relations

Steven Spano—Plumbing, Owner

Tommy Moran—United Parcel Service

Tom Pellicano—Education

Tom Tibaldi—Lawyer

Tony Soscia—Lawyer

* *The names above represent families that lived in or near the Gun Hill projects in the '50s, '60s, '70s, and beyond. There are some dear family members and friends who have passed away, but their spirits live on.*

NOTES

PREFACE

Paula Fromby and Andrew Cherlin, in their article, "Family Instability and Child Well-Being," note, "The instability of family structure has become an increasingly salient part of children's lives in the United States over the past half-century. During this period, as is well-known, divorce rates increased ... experience transitions into single parent families ..." Additionally, they highlight, "Having an intact family provides a key framework within which childhood development occurs ... family structure change ... and major negative life events."[74]

CHAPTER 3: SOCIAL SUPPORT

Social support represents the community framework that balances the primary structure within the family. Children can thrive and gain extraordinary self-confidence when caring leaders embrace and encourage the well-being of those they lead.

---

[74] *Am Social Rev.* 72, no. 2 (April 2007): 181–204.

CHAPTER 4: EDUCATIONAL INFLUENCE

The multiple layers of education that our young receive have a profound impact on the development of their psyches. Our educators, as well of the educational system, must be consistently vigilant and ensure that all children receive the best of care from the most-qualified teachers available. All children have the capacity to learn, and it takes thoughtful, patient instructors who provide educational enrichment to keep students motivated.

CHAPTER 8: EXPERIENTIAL LEARNING

Learning through life experiences is a meaningful and timeless process. There is no greater vehicle than life's experiences to entrench understanding. As an example, many educational formats now embrace the concept of experiential learning, with student engagement as a method of enhancing understanding. Learning through trial and error can be enlightening and fulfilling experiences that serve to motivate individuals to progress. Experiential learning builds confidence and promotes a desire to seek and interpret new information. Expanding our reservoir of thoughts and emotions will go a long way toward strengthening the human experience.

CHAPTER 10: REGENERATION

For additional information on US Census data (2014) linked to children living with two parents into adulthood across the educational and racial spectrum, see the following: https://ifstudies.org/blog/more-than-60-of-u-s-kids-live-with-two-biological-parents.

SOURCES

Anderson, Dr. Jane. "The Impact of Family Structure on the Health of Children: Effects of Divorce." https://www.ncbi.nlm.nih.gov/pmc/articles/PMC4240051/.

Bloom, Dr. Benjamin. *Developing Talent in Young People.* Random House, 1985.

Centers for Medicare and Medicaid Services. https://www.cms.gov/Research-Statistics-Data-and-Systems/Statistics-Trends-and Reports/NationalHealthExpendData/NationalHealth AccountsHistorical.html.

Chetty, Raj et al. "Where Is the Land of Opportunity? The Geography of Intergenerational Mobility in the United States." http://nber.org/papers/w19843.

Fagan, Patrick, and Christina Hadford. *The Fifth Annual Index of Family Belonging and Rejection.* http://marri.us/research/research-papers/fifth-annual-index-of-belonging-and-rejection.

FamilyFacts.org.

"Family values." http://www. dictionary.com.

"Family values." http://www.merriam-webster.com.

"Family values." https://www.oxforddictionaries.com.

Fromby, Paula, and Andrew Cherlin. "Family Instability and Child Well-Being." *Am Social Rev.* 72, no. 2 (April 2007).

Gladwell, Malcolm. *Tipping Point: How Little Things Can Make a Big Difference.* Little, Brown and Company, 2000.

Goleman, Daniel. *Working with Emotional Intelligence.* Bantam Books, 1998.

Harari, Oren. *The Leadership Secrets of Colin Powell.* McGraw Hill, 2002.

Heinrich, Carolyn J. "Parents' Employment and Children's Well-Being." https://pdfs.semanticscholar.org/6a30/12e9f7bd125f9faff979 0ee79be9a698d871.pdf.

http://infohub.nyced.org/reports-and-policies/citywide-information-and-data/graduation-results.

http://medium.com/2016-index-of-culture-and-opportunity/divorce-in-our-nation-b2f69db56872.

http://psychcentral.com/news/2015/12/23/parents-touch-support-play-vital-to-kids-happiness-as-adults/96613.html.

http://schools.nyc.gov.

http://www.bookbrowse.com/expressions/detail/index.cfm/expression_number/446/laugh-and-the-world-laughs -with-you-weep-and-you-weep-alone.

http://www.nccp.org/topics/childpoverty.html.

http://www.nycenet.edu/offices/finance_schools/budget/DSBPO/allocationmemo/fy18_19/FY19_docs/FY2019_FSF_Guide.pdf.

http://www.thepublicdiscourse.com/2015/12/15983/
thepublicdiscourse.com; the Witherspoon institute, Glenn Stanton,
12/16/2015.

Kaiser Family Foundation. 2010 National Health Expenditures. http://
www.cms.hhs.gov/NationalHealthExpendData.

Kotter, John P. *Leading Change.* Harvard Business Press, 1996.

Mangione, Jerre, and Ben Morreale. *La Storia: Five Centuries of the Italian
American Experience.* HarperCollins Publishers, 1992.

National Health Expenditures. http://www.cms.hhs.gov/National
HealthExpendData/.

NCHS, National Health and Nutrition Examination Survey (NHANES).
http://www.cdc.gov/nchs/hus/contents2016.htm#fig15.

NCHS, National Health and Nutrition Examination Survey (NHANES).
http://www.cdc.gov/nchs/hus/contents2016.htm#fig06.

No Isolation. "Social Behaviour." https://www.noisolation.com/
global/research/how-does-social-isolation-affect-a-childs-mental-
health-and-development.

Rector, Robert. "Marriage: America's Greatest Weapon against
Child Poverty." https://www.heritage.org/poverty-and-inequality/
report/marriage-americas-greatest-weapon-against-child-poverty

Resurgenceblog.wordpress.com/2012/11/11/seeking-recognition-and-
approval-are-we-looking- in-the-right-places.

"Retail Prices of Food, 1964–68, Indexes and Average Prices," Bulletin
of the US Bureau of Labor Statistics, no. 1632. https://fraser.
stlouisfed.org/files/docs/publications/bls/bls_1632_1969.pdf.

Schwartz, Barry. *Why We Work.* Simon & Schuster, 2015.

Secunda, Victoria. *Losing Your Parents, Finding Your Self.* Hyperion, 2000.

Stanton, Glenn. http://www.thepublicdiscourse.com/2015/12/15983.

US Census Bureau, Statistical Abstract of the United States, 2011. https://www2.census.gov/library/publications/2010/compendia/statab/130ed/tables/vitstat.pdf.

www.countyhealthrankings.org/app/new-york/2017/measure/factors/82/data?sort=desc-0.

ABOUT THE AUTHOR

Gerard Azzari was born and raised in the Gun Hill housing projects in the Bronx, New York, and is the youngest of five children. His education and employment took root primarily in the Bronx and Manhattan. Gerard earned his bachelor of science degree in biology from Fordham University. He also attended New York Medical College for basic medical science and completed executive-level dynamic leadership training from Columbia University Graduate School of Business.

He developed unique insights into individual and group dynamics, having lived in a low-income urban setting for more than twenty years. With more than thirty years of experience in the social service and pharmaceutical arenas, he is acutely aware of the importance of leadership and accountability in guiding individuals to achieve success.

Gerard is a results-driven sales executive with extensive experience in United States and international sales, sales management, training, development, and human resources.

He is recognized for his exceptional interpersonal and motivational skills, business acumen, sound judgment, and ability to achieve consistent results. He is passionate about raising awareness of the need for greater parental guidance in leading children to become capable adults.

Gerard attributes any success earned as a direct result of childhood learning from his faith, family, education, mentors, friends, and environment.

In addition to his executive-sales consulting responsibilities, he maintains an active schedule of community activities with his wife and children. He enjoys providing support for services linked to youth development and athletics, as well as speaking on motivational topics.

INDEX

D

death's value vii, 103, 113
devotion xvii, 65, 104, 136
discipline xi, 2, 5, 11, 17, 30, 37, 38, 39,
    42, 43, 46, 61, 92, 101

E

educational erosion xxv
educational influence vii, 41, 42, 174
educational system xi, xv, 26, 41, 55,
    73, 127, 174
effort xxv, xxvi, 11, 15, 21, 25, 26, 29,
    31, 32, 33, 34, 35, 37, 43, 44, 45,
    46, 50, 51, 54, 55, 60, 63, 64, 66,
    68, 73, 77, 79, 80, 83, 85, 100, 105,
    107, 108, 109, 110, 112, 116, 118,
    125, 128, 129, 136, 137
emotional intelligence 90, 91, 176
employment xiv, 5, 6, 7, 8, 9, 25, 33, 37,
    43, 49, 56, 57, 68, 78, 81, 83, 84,
    87, 91, 97, 120, 125, 176, 179
experiential learning vii, xxi, 47, 51, 61,
    89, 95, 100, 101, 174

F

faith and family vii, xxv, 17
family-based culture 126
family values vii, xii, xiii, 17, 18, 19, 24,
    97, 126, 175, 176
father vii, xiv, 1, 4, 5, 6, 7, 8, 9, 13, 14,
    18, 43, 47, 64, 66, 67, 72, 77, 79,
    87, 96, 104, 105, 106, 107, 108,
    119, 120
Fordham University 9, 37, 46, 50, 69,
    79, 85, 151, 160, 179
freedom of choice xxv
friends xi, xv, xvii, xx, xxv, 2, 3, 4, 5, 8,
    10, 11, 14, 16, 21, 23, 25, 27, 28,
    29, 30, 31, 32, 33, 35, 36, 37, 42,
    46, 47, 51, 55, 56, 57, 59, 60, 65,
    66, 68, 71, 82, 83, 85, 86, 88, 89,
    92, 97, 98, 105, 106, 108, 110, 121,
    128, 135, 171, 180
friendships 10, 24, 39, 46, 50, 65, 66, 67,
    68, 69, 83, 90, 97, 105

G

golden rule 19
governmental disorder xxv
grateful xi, xvii, 68, 93
Gun Hill housing projects 2, 19,
    105, 179
Gun Hill Road 9, 10, 147, 149

H

harmony xxiv, 20, 39, 66, 77, 104, 136
hope xxv, xxvi, 74

I

intact families xi, xiv, 73, 117, 119,
    123, 125
integrity 24, 34, 68, 73, 74, 81, 136

K

kindness xxiii, xxiv

L

laughter 15, 66, 68, 69
leadership xxi, 32, 51, 56, 57, 58, 83,
    87, 88, 89, 91, 92, 93, 97, 111,
    124, 129, 130, 131, 132, 136, 176,
    179, 180
learning vii, xi, xiv, xx, xxi, 1, 3, 4, 10,
    11, 15, 25, 30, 31, 32, 35, 41, 42,
    43, 44, 45, 46, 47, 49, 51, 54, 56,
    58, 61, 64, 65, 68, 71, 74, 76, 79,
    80, 83, 85, 89, 91, 95, 97, 99, 100,
    101, 115, 116, 121, 125, 128, 135,
    136, 174, 180
logic iii, v, xxi, 14, 72, 90, 116, 136